Apostolic Style
and
Lutheran Substance

Ten Years Of Controversy
Over What Can Change

An Update On The Book

Evangelical Style and Lutheran Substance

David S. Luecke

Fairway Press, Lima, Ohio

APOSTOLIC STYLE AND LUTHERAN SUBSTANCE

THIRD PRINTING 2004

SECOND PRINTING 2001

FIRST EDITION
Copyright © 1999 by
David S. Luecke

Library of Congress Control Number: 00-130406

ISBN 0-7880-1623-7   PRINTED IN U.S.A.

Books by David S. Luecke

Pastoral Administration:
*Integrating Ministry and Management,**
with Samuel Southard, Word 1986

Evangelical Style and Lutheran Substance:
*Facing America's Mission Challenge,**
Concordia Publishing House 1988

*New Designs for Church Leadership**
Concordia Publishing House 1990

Courageous Churches:
Refusing Decline Inviting Growth
with Kent Hunter, Concordia Publishing House 1991

The Other Story of Lutherans at Worship:
*Reclaiming Our Heritage of Diversity**
Fellowship Ministries 1995

Talking With God:
*How Ordinary Christians Grow in Prayer**
Fellowship Ministries 1997

*Available from Fairway Press

Contents

Dedicated to

Rev. James P. Martin

This book would not have happened without the encouragement and support of Rev. James P. Martin, Senior Pastor of Royal Redeemer Lutheran Church in North Royalton, Ohio. He first suggested the idea of a ten-year follow up to *Evangelical Style and Lutheran Substance.*

He was the moving force behind the neighboring new church that I was called to plant in 1990. Without his steady support Community of Hope would not now have its own building. He invited me to become Administrative Pastor at Royal Redeemer and insisted that I have the time to be in ministry to other congregations and to the church at large.

Jim is showing me what a passion for the lost looks like month-by-month and how the courage to pursue this mission works its way out year-by-year in the decision-making processes of a congregation. With him I am seeing new dimensions of what can happen in a congregation through a philosophy of ministry that challenges all members to be ministers. His special spiritual gift of discerning what new ventures God is ready to bless is deepening my understanding of God's presence and power in his church.

Infectious church growth was my concern when I wrote the book ten years ago. Thanks to Jim Martin, I am now ministering in the middle of it. What a special privilege!

CHAPTER 1

Introduction

"Regaining An Infectious Spirit" was the working title of the book that became *Evangelical Style and Lutheran Substance*. It was a last minute change by the editorial committee that approved publication. Actually they wanted Evangelical Style and <u>Mainline</u> Substance, but I pleaded not to add the burden of association with dying liberal mainline churches. <u>Lutheran</u> substance it became.

Ten years later a better title would be Apostolic Style and Lutheran Substance, as I will explain.

The combinations of substance/style and Lutheran/Evangelical hit a nerve and brought strong reaction. Much of it was favorable and led to invitations to present the concepts at twenty district and national conferences, including the Council of Presidents of The Lutheran Church—Missouri Synod. Eight of these events involved dialogue with seminary faculty representatives of the growing opposition to anything labeled Church Growth.

For complicated reasons, those opposition forces prevailed in the national politics of the Lutheran Church—Missouri Synod. In the mid-1990s the Great Church Growth Debate died, and with it discussions of substance and style. One CPH catalogue listed four publications of mine; the next year had none. The book that sold over 6,500 copies went out of print.

Ten years later the issues have not gone away. Within the Lutheran Church—Missouri Synod, the gap has widened between those pursuing changes in styles of ministry and those insisting there is nothing wrong with any part of the inherited tradition. In the absence of organized dialogue, the positions have hardened more noticeably between the doers at the congregational level and the teachers/authorities at the synodical level.

Ten years later I understand the issues better. I have experienced how hot are the topics of worship, office of public ministry, and Evangelical influence. I recognize more thoroughly the fears of practicing pastors. I can better recognize and deal with a widespread reluctance to do careful analysis of strengths, weaknesses, and history of church life. I can offer better explanation for why the sides keep talking past each other. I now know more, having researched and written a book on each of three major topics at issue: worship, prayer, and church organization. And, the Holy Spirit has had ten more years to work on me.

In Chapters 2-8 that follow, I will attempt to sharpen thinking about the major issues based on ten more years of experience. Chapters 9-12 focus more intently on the same bottom-line proposals of the book ten years ago: Lutherans can and should learn how better to communicate and organize.

The first book developed out of an invitation in 1985 to share with synodical mission executives what I was learning from Evangelicals through my experience as administrator and faculty member at Fuller Theological Seminary in Pasadena, California, often regarded as the flagship of Evangelical seminaries. I saw myself as an explorer sending back reports from a different part of the world.

Recently I was visiting with pastors of a neighboring circuit in the Cleveland area. Conversation turned to a nearby fast-growing community church that went from 0 to attendance of 750 in six years. One of the pastors wondered, "What do people find there?" I replied, "That is what I was wondering when I wrote *Evangelical Style and Lutheran Substance*." Indeed the fast-growing Evangelical churches in Southern California were the natives I was reporting on. How do fast-growing Evangelical churches still do that all over America?

FOUR ADMIRABLE STYLES OF COMMUNICATING AND ORGANIZING

Ten years ago I saw four admirable features of fast-growing Evangelical churches that traditional congregations could explore and consider adapting to their own ministries.

1. Better Audience Contact

One way to describe Evangelicals is audience centered. They tend to be passionate about communicating a message. This can be recognized any day on religious radio or television anywhere in the country. The number of their stations and programs grew even more in the last ten years.

To me this is something to be admired. Evangelicals have certainly learned how to communicate with ordinary people. They have more of the apostolic style shown by Paul, who could talk to traditional synagogue Jews in Hebrew (Acts 17:2-3), appeal to university elitists in Greek (Acts 17:22-31), and slip into the common man's Aramaic dialect (Acts 22:2-21), telling his born-again story. One key is willingness to be personal.

Another is high priority given to expecting audience response, which is the basis to good communication.

The action step I recommend is that leaders should stay close to their audience. This seems simple enough, but it has tremendous implications for planning worship. The tradition of Lutheran worship leaders is to be proclaimers rather than communicators. The tradition puts distance between them and the congregation as audience—by the clothes they wear, the formalities they rely on, the specialized language they use, the distant pulpit they stand behind, the ritual they enact, the unusual songs they choose, and even their readiness to turn their back on the audience. The tradition takes the congregation for granted. The Apostle Paul, for one, worked hard to build his audiences.

The additional focus on audience contact in this book recognizes the informality and spontaneity of communication in the worship of New Testament apostolic churches. I offer data that show a general decline of emphasis on preaching in Lutheran churches in recent decades. Meanwhile, the emphasis on the sacrament of the Lord's Supper has increased, moving from quarterly celebration a century ago to the present norm of weekly celebration in one or all services. There is danger in these twin developments. Our Lutheran forefathers would want assurances that Lutheran congregations today are not guilty of what to them was fundamentally unLutheran: sacramentalism. Lutherans have historically maintained that the preached Word should take precedence over the sacraments. Is such a priority still the common practice?

2. More Personal Faith Expressions

Also to be admired are ordinary church goers who talk openly and freely about their faith with one another. Such faith talk communicates spiritual life better than the social small talk Lutherans usually fall into even in churchly settings.

Lutherans could be more willing to bless simple faith talk, even when it is immature. We could share more discussion of our individual personal spiritual journeys. We could try to become bilingual, adding the language of personal experience to the propositional language of doctrine we are raised on.

Probably the easiest way to get traditional Lutherans more comfortable sharing their faith with others is to engage them in sharing prayers of personal conversation with God. To concentrate on enriching the fellowship life through shared personal prayer is a style improvement that seems the most practical step toward more infectious faith talk.

The last ten years have witnessed increased involvement of members in the visible prayer life of many Lutheran congregations, as is most apparent in the growing number of churches that have organized prayer chains. Worrisome, though, is increased acceptance and club-like use in some liturgical circles of a medieval principle that warns against errors in prayer that may lead to errors in faith; therefore, Lutherans should not pray in their own words because they may say something wrong. The same questionable principle is used to justify insistence on only hymnal-approved worship rites.

3. More Movement-Style Of Organizing

Organizing at the grassroots level is how the apostles went about building churches. Evangelicals seem adept at doing that today, with relatively independent congregations and independent para-church organizations that have to stay close to their grass-roots constituencies. In contrast, the Lutheran heritage for most of its history was definitely top down. Centralized authority served Lutherans well in this country all the way through the great church-planting boom after the Second World War. It does not seem as productive now.

Some apostolic, Evangelical emphases that can be highlighted in Lutheran organizing are:

a) Structure around groups of people participating in the primary fellowship of Word, prayer and support rather than around organizational boards and committees.

b) Accentuate local church initiatives, which is where the action is and thus where productive ministry innovations come from. This is more difficult for the ELCA to do because of the hierarchical polity chosen for the merged synod and national organizations. Missouri Synod can recover more of the strengths of the congregational polity basic to its formation 150 years ago.

c) Affirm para-church organizations, which usually start up with the initiative of strong-willed lay people. Lutheran congregations are getting increasingly comfortable tapping into the resources of non-synodical, special purpose ministry organizations.

d) Recognize the blessing of diversity. Uniformity among and within Lutheran churches worked through the 1960s. Churches now are

10

learning how to recognize and build on diversity. The Apostle Paul blessed such diversity with powerful theological rationale.

4. Better Recognition That Everyone Is A Minister

Those statements of Paul focus on how God through the Holy Spirit raises up people in the church with a range of giftedness to contribute to the common good. Growing churches today are learning how to organize more informally around giftedness rather than formally around positions and credentials. Inevitably this approach relies heavily on lay ministry. Lutherans have two traditions of ministry. The narrow one keeps the authority and responsibility for ministry focused on the credentialed pastor. The broad one spreads the tasks of ministry widely among lay people, with the pastor functioning more as teacher and coach.

Reviving the Lutheran tradition of broad ministry means:
a) Expect widespread leadership initiatives by returning ministry to the laity, and in the process de-emphasize the sharp distinction between clergy and laity.
b) Ease access to ministry positions, both lay and credentialed ministry.
c) Be less reliant on organizational solutions. Lutherans seem instinctively to resist the possibility of confusion by organizing to prevent it. But we often then miss valuable spiritual initiatives that do not fit the formal organization in place. We can learn to be more tolerant of ambiguity.
d) Expect strong pastoral leadership. More lay ministry does not need to weaken pastoral leadership. It can increase the amount of influence in congregational life and therefore give more for the pastor to lead.

CAN OLD CHURCHES ADAPT NEW STYLES?

The introductory part of *Evangelical Style and Lutheran Substance* posed questions for old churches. Old are not only congregations that have been around for generations but also church bodies that remember and rely on their historical roots in Europe, like Presbyterians, Episcopalians, Congregationalists—and Lutherans. Old church bodies, often identified as mainline, are declining. The growing church bodies are mostly the ones coming from the American experience in the last century and a half, like

Baptists, Assemblies of God, Seventh Day Adventists, and, in the last twenty years, Vineyard.

Evangelism seems easy for congregations with infectious growth. Participants invite friends and they come. Evangelism seems hard for most Lutherans. Members too often do not invite friends, and when they do, those invitations too often are left unanswered. Why?

The basic difficulty of old churches is their tendency to lose their sense of expectancy, to think they have discovered everything that is important. Their rich past encourages them to look backward rather than to follow Christ forward into the new forms and styles of ministry he seems to be blessing in a new generation.

When considering churches with infectious growth, Lutheran church leaders might ask themselves these questions: What can we learn? What can we change? What can we share with others? What is the course of faithfulness in mixing innovation and preservation? Where is the dividing line between laudable adaptation of outreach style and necessary protection of unchangeable theological substance? How important is church growth?

The first apostolic convention, reported in Acts 15, had to sort out changes that were happening as Gentiles became part of the new Christian church that was until then mostly Jewish. The apostles set the precedent for drawing a line between what can be called unchangeable substance and what amounts to styles of expressing it that can change.

Declining old churches need new vision. Exploring what growing churches are doing today is good preparation for something that ultimately the Holy Spirit has to grant. Also good preparation is renewed commitment to a theology of the cross—readiness to live totally by faith and willingness to lose old church life in order to save it. Denying self to follow Jesus translates into readiness to take risk when choosing a course between preservation and innovation.

BORROWING AND ADAPTING STYLES

At Pentecost the apostles set a model for ministry when, moved by the Holy Spirit, they found themselves talking languages new to them. They spoke so convincingly that hearers from many different cultural backgrounds could say, "How is it that each of us hears them in his own native language?" The apostles borrowed languages to customize their message. They used many styles to communicate the same substance.

12

Basic to a church's style are customary ways to hold up Christ for others to see and ways to wait upon the Holy Spirit.

"Waiting upon the Spirit" describes basic spirituality. The apostles were prepared to recognize the presence and work of the Holy Spirit, imparted by God's grace, as directly as possible. Evangelicals keep a focus on such experiences, especially that of being born again. Through the Word, the Holy Spirit is present among Lutherans, too, but our style tends to make him hard to recognize, and we do not expect him to move us so openly and forcefully.

"How Christ is held up" in church life inquires about what dimensions of his past and current presence are featured. How is his redeeming work presented? Those to be reached have to be able to recognize him and the differences he makes in ways they understand and feel. Because of their distinct culture, Lutherans are prone to raise up Christ in ways that do not get the attention of people different from ourselves. The key is understanding and addressing needs they feel and recognize.

Marketing is a modern term for the focus on trying to understand what potential consumers want when they are shopping to fill their needs. Starting with consumer insights, marketers help shape and package the product offering so that it has a better chance of getting attention and acceptance. Starting with the product, engineers are technical experts who tend to start with what they know is the best design. But in this consumer society, there are many examples of excellently designed product offerings that found few consumers.

The Lutheran heritage is first-rate theological engineering that proclaims the Word of God in all its depth and breadth. If the Gospel were an automobile in the 1960s, Lutherans would be the Volkswagen of the industry. VW "beetles" were well-designed cars that were once well appreciated in America. The fact of the marketplace, however, is that Volkswagen lost considerable market share in this country in recent decades. Competitors paid more attention to features that car buyers grew to expect. Only in recent years have marketers been added to the engineer-dominated upper levels of VW corporate management. Their sales are now improving.

Churches do not have to force choice between either engineering or marketing, between presenting theological expertise or innovatively addressing felt needs. The best is both/and. Churches that sustain infectious growth have usually found such a combination.

Lutherans do share more of a common history with American Evangelicals than is commonly recognized today. The German version of eighteenth century revivals in Britain and its American colonies was called pietism. In the nineteenth century The Lutheran Church—Missouri Synod was founded by leaders who continued in America the pietist Awakening Movement they were part of in Germany. Those pietist roots are remembered now mostly in exaggerated caricature of its weaknesses, but the strengths of this piety continued in this church body well into the twentieth century. In British tradition, German pietist excesses would have been recognized and set aside as Arminian theology. That danger is explained further in Chapter 4.

APOSTOLIC STYLE

We can talk about "catholic" as styles developed in the universal, catholic church over all the centuries between the first and the present. Catholic leanings among many church professionals in the LCMS have gone so far that "Evangelical style" now meets with derision, disdain, and blind resistance. Lay members and leaders in the LCMS, on the other hand, are generally more attracted to "Evangelical" styles that are so well communicated in the popular Christian culture of America today.

In writing this book's chapter on borrowing from Evangelicals or from Catholics, I slowly realized that a basic difference between these perspectives is historical focus. "Catholic" in Lutheran circles today means universal church, with a current focus on fourth-century Christianity and medieval monastic practices, along with the necessary Lutheran preoccupation with the sixteenth century. Evangelicals, in contrast, typically jump from today right to the Biblical first century, without many stops in-between. To Catholics the church of Bible times represents the "primitive" church. To Evangelicals it is the "early" church, the church of the apostles.

I trust that raising up first-century "apostolic style" will receive a broader hearing today, especially from Lutherans who balk at things Evangelical. The four styles of communicating and organizing featured in this and the earlier book have clear Biblical roots. For Lutherans many church traditions accumulated after the Biblical first century at one time may well have been productive practices consistent with Scripture. The Reformation century remains of necessity important to Lutherans. But when a church body's traditions are losing effectiveness, to go back directly to church styles of the apostles makes more sense than to try to adapt traditions from yet other centuries between then and now.

The next seven chapters make up Part I, How the Issues Look After Ten Years. These chapters present my take on the issues most basic to the controversy among pastors, seminary professors, and officials specifically of The Lutheran Church—Missouri Synod: — How do we regain an infectious Spirit? Can there be different styles for the same substance? Should we borrow from Evangelicals or from Catholics? What should be the relationship between sociology and theology in understanding church life? Is church culture a means or an end? Is our ministry to the weak or to the strong? What is the Lutheran substance?

Part II, Better Ways of Communicating and Organizing, presents the four admirable styles that Lutherans could productively adapt. The discussion identifies their roots in the writings of the apostles.

PART I

How The Issues Look
Ten Years Later

CHAPTER 2

Regaining An Infectious Spirit

The book ten years ago had the theme "Regaining An Infectious Spirit." That kind of spirit was apparent among many growing Lutheran churches in the nineteenth century and again more recently in the 1950s. The theme of an infectious spirit carries recognition that in churches such a human spirit is dependent on the work of the Holy Spirit. A reasonable question is: What can we learn from how Word and sacraments are used when and where the Holy Spirit seems to be working best in congregations today? The place to look is churches that are "infectious" now, not thirty or a hundred years ago. Today in America such churches are mostly Evangelical in orientation. They communicate and organize in distinctive ways from which Lutherans can learn.

I focus on the Holy Spirit because something strange happened in the church growth discussions among some Lutherans in the early 1990s. In addition to their insistence that nothing can be learned from Evangelical churches, the vocal opponents oversimplified the issues and charged that "church growthers" expected to build churches by relying on techniques and not on God. If true, such an emphasis indeed deserved to be dismissed as a passing fad.

The Holy Spirit remains the power who calls and gathers, as well as enlightens and sanctifies the whole Christian church on earth. This confession of Luther is a great encouragement for church builders all too aware of their human limitations—but also a great frustration. Why are some efforts blessed with expanding impact, while others are not? It's the same question that applies to hearers of the Gospel: Why do some get it and others just like them do not? The only lasting explanation is to hear Jesus compare the Holy Spirit to the wind that blows wherever it pleases. We can hear the wind's sound and see its impact, but we cannot confidently predict where the Spirit will touch down with unusual force.

This is not to say that church leaders are without clues. Clearly the Word of God is to be presented in all its depth and strength. But the Spirit seems to have more impact today where the Word is communicated in styles that strive to find new audiences and to hold their attention. The Spirit seems better able to work where many participants, not just the church professionals, are continually relating the Gospel to others through personal

19

faith expressions. The Spirit seems to operate most readily today through primary informal fellowship groups and local church initiatives that recognize diversity among participants. The Spirit seems to have expanding impact in churches with extensive lay involvement in ministry.

That's pretty much the message of Apostolic style for Lutherans, whose traditions often work against these styles of ministry.

DISCOVERIES

Will better ways of talking and organizing guarantee results? Apparently not. Hundreds of church leaders can tell stories of good human church-growth efforts that yielded little recognizable growth. There is a difference between observing, on the one hand, that most growing churches have certain characteristics and claiming, on the other hand, that most churches with those characteristics will grow. That difference is the unpredictable Holy Spirit, who will not be confined to a set of techniques. Thank God for making his transcendence apparent.

Ten years later I know more but also less about church growth than I did before. In 1990 I accepted a call from the Ohio District of the LCMS to plant a church in a southern suburb of Cleveland. I wanted to try out some ministry styles and see "up close" what happens—a motivation that is not the best for starting a church. I know less about techniques that work because everything I tried worked a little, but none worked a lot. I know more about dependence on God for his blessings on church growth efforts.

One lesson learned is the difficulty of changing church culture, even among Lutherans who are open to change. There is a difference between trying something new and having the confidence and experience to do it well.

Another discovery is how dependence on the Holy Spirit works month by month in the development of a congregation. The Spirit works through a new mother reached by just one more canvas call, who a year later shows up and adds new life to the church music. The Spirit works through a woman responding to a newspaper article who eventually brings others that model prayer and personal faith expressions. The Spirit is at work in a newly retired mature Lutheran church leader who accepts the challenge to help start a church and who year by year guides it through one difficulty after another. My point is that the Holy Spirit works through specific personalities. What they happen to bring to the church community determines a lot of the congregation's character and potential.

My parallel point is that much of a congregation's future is determined through individuals who were approached but did not show up. They may be people who could have a big community impact but do not respond to mailings or "Bring a Friend" invitations. The "no shows" may be seekers who could come alive in Christ and spread their enthusiasm to others. One can think of all sorts of personalities who might make a big difference in a church's development. Whether or not they respond is determined ultimately by the Holy Spirit, who does the real calling and gathering through the people already called and gathered.

Clearly the personality, energy and skills of the church planter have a lot to do with what emerges. But not all. My efforts brought at best modest outcomes at Community of Hope—attendance of about 60 in a building of our own, with encouraging spiritual dynamics and some neat stories of personal growth in Christ. But we were still waiting for an infectious spirit of growth. Maybe that will happen with their new leader.

Meanwhile God has moved me on to the larger neighboring congregation, Royal Redeemer, as part of a team aggressively committed to church growth in that community. In God's providence, I am now privileged to be part of a church that does have an infectious spirit of growth. In the last five years attendance increased 60% to the present average of 900.

From this vantage point I can offer two more first-hand observations about how churches grow. One is the realization that the Holy Spirit still does his work through specific personalities and through what looks a lot like "happenstance." New programs flourish when the right staff or volunteer leaders emerge; they wither and die without them. The Spirit gets his work done through a new religion editor of the Cleveland newspaper who does a feature on churches with contemporary worship and highlights Royal Redeemer with a big picture on the front page of the Sunday issue. Attendance rose a hundred in the following month and continues to rise.

The other observation is that, while church leaders cannot on their own produce an infectious church spirit, they need to be good stewards to avoid turning one off. Not expanding facilities or adding staff can choke growth dynamics. In Royal Redeemer's experience the additions have preceded the growth in numbers necessary to pay for them. This means taking financial risks year after year. My colleague, Pastor Jim Martin, seems especially gifted to discern and cast a vision for what God is ready to bless. Again and again God works in ways that force us to recognize our dependence on Him.

Of the four styles of communicating and organizing highlighted in the first book and again in this one, Royal Redeemer is well on the way with engaging worship, informal group-oriented organizing, and widespread lay involvement in doing ministry. Efforts to facilitate more shared prayer have not had much impact yet. Maybe next year.

AN INFECTIOUS SPIRIT REGAINED?

Many Lutheran churches have had infectious growth in the past. This was especially true in the nineteenth century for churches in this country that developed ministry styles appealing to immigrants from Germany and Scandinavia. Much of that style, including language, had changed by the time of the church growth spurt accompanying the widespread move to suburbia in the decades right after World War II. Worship was formalized and upgraded, uniformity was respected, and church-wide programs brought exciting outcomes. But times change. Beginning in the late 1960s mainline denominations with long traditions went into a decline that still continues for most.

Has such an infectious spirit been regained among Lutherans?

No and Yes.

The main news for Lutheran churches is continued decline, although the rate is slowing down. In the Lutheran Church—Missouri Synod total baptized membership dropped 3.85% from 1987 to 1997. The drop in confirmed membership was an even greater 4.42%.

Meanwhile the attention to numbers has widely shifted from membership lists to average attendance at worship. Interesting in itself is how quickly came this recognition that worship attendance is a much better indicator of congregational vitality than reports that may include many members who drifted away without saying so.

In the years between 1987 and 1997 average weekly attendance in the LCMS grew—in 23% of the congregations. It decreased in 52%. In this statistic growth or decline in attendance meant having a change of 10% or more over those ten years. The average attendance among all LCMS congregations went from 173 in 1987 to 155 in 1997.

There is reason to suspect the decline is even greater, since many more congregations no longer even update their annual statistics. Recently the figure of non-reporters has been about 30%, compared to only 7% ten years ago.

An infectious spirit that brings growth has not become common in the LCMS.

Growth In Large Congregations

Yet it is present in a small but growing number of congregations. Assume for this purpose that a congregation that has 35 or more adult confirmations a year is showing symptoms of infectiousness in their outreach. This count does not include transfers from other Lutheran congregations, which reflect a different kind of growth. Ten years ago the number of congregations reporting 35 or more adult confirmations was less than 50. In the last several years that count is approaching 100.

Three trends underlie this shift. A church with so many adult confirmands is probably big or on the way to becoming big. Given declining membership of the whole church body, this means the growth is with big churches. They are compensating for broad-based decline in small and medium sized churches. Roughly half of all LCMS congregations yearly report no adult confirmation, or only one.

Secondly, the rise of large Lutheran churches reflects the growing importance of mega churches in general as centers of infectious growth among Protestants. Widespread use of the new term "mega" is itself a development of the last decade or so. Increasingly people prefer to pursue their spiritual life in large churches. The usual explanation is the greater diversity of offerings that are well done and that provide better opportunity to find community with others of similar age, interests, and needs. Finding a diversity of styles within the same congregation has risen in importance.

This situation is quite different from the fast church-body growth of the late 1940s through the early 60s, which mainly involved widespread planting of churches in the new suburbs. In that period LCMS congregations increased from about 4,500 to nearly 6,000. A total that has not changed more than three percent since. Uniformity was welcomed then as reassurance that the new congregation was not substantially different from the old church that had served them well. Suburbanites then tended to be of similar age, background, and interests. Most of those suburban churches remained small.

A third trend is for current Lutheran mega churches to be different from other Lutheran congregations. This is only partly a matter of size. Most are also different from the Lutheran congregations that grew large in the ethnic communities of previous generations. What distinguishes many of them is openness to and support of a wide range of spiritual backgrounds, needs, and preferences among the participants, and then the ability to handle the resulting complexity. Ethnic congregations were largely intolerant of diversity, and the willing conformity of participants made such churches simple enough for one pastor to handle memberships of 1,000 or more.

23

The dominant path to infectious growth today is to move beyond expecting conformity to tolerating diversity, and then to welcoming and being able to support spiritual seekers who may be very different from one another and from traditional Lutherans. Mega churches typically have developed a church culture that is distinctive in ways beyond size.

Fundamental to making this transition is the ability to distinguish changeable style from unchanging substance.

The Lutheran mega church pastors I know would insist that their preaching and teaching remains solidly Lutheran. Many of the churches and pastors that annually do confirm 35 or more adults became familiar to me through a study of several hundred LCMS churches. That study turned into the analysis of the 50 congregations reported in Courageous Churches, a book that Kent Hunter and I authored in 1991. I have maintained contact with many through correspondence and conferences.

The Unpredictable Holy Spirit

An infectious spirit of growth remains dependent on the unpredictable movement of the Holy Spirit, especially in churches that have moved beyond ethnic conformity. Is it possible to plant churches that are targeted to grow into the mega category? There have been several Lutheran denominational attempts to test an approach that amounts to a reliance on techniques and informed, well-motivated human effort. One highly visible Lutheran mega church tried a well-funded franchise duplication of itself in other metropolitan areas. The results were disappointing, and one hears little such talk of "franchising" anymore. The other attempt was to annually convene a Mega Church Conference, with the obvious intent to facilitate growth of mega churches. Fine things happened for many participating pastors. But the name has wisely been changed to the Growing Churches Conference.

Explanation for why it is hard purposely to incubate or cause sustained infectious growth can be seen in observations from the large-scale Church Membership Initiative study of Lutheran churches reported in 1993. Churches grow each in their own way, one by one. Their principal common denominators are 1) the desire of leaders to see growth happen and 2) the willingness to make the uncomfortable changes involved in adjusting to new diversity. Also, most stories of unusual growth have some sort of significant "igniter event" unique to that congregation and community. Their pastors and church leaders were able to capitalize on the dynamics set off by this event, which often was not something planned. Therein is the work of the Holy Spirit most readily to be seen.

24

CHAPTER 3

Different Styles For
The Same Substance?

The distinction between substance and style seems intuitively appropriate and helpful. In Scripture this distinction can be found in the work of the first apostolic convention, as recorded in Acts 15. In the shift from Jewish to Gentile cultures, they drew a line between what could change in church life and what could not. It was no longer necessary to be a circumcised Jew in order to be a Christian. Chairman James announced the conclusion with these words, "We should not make it difficult for the Gentiles who are turning to God."

Does a person have to fit into a distict Lutheran culture in order to be a Lutheran Christian? Not historically. Language is basic to a culture, and Christians can be Lutheran without speaking German (or Swedish, Norwegian, Danish, Finnish or Slovak). That cultural change of language was successfully negotiated in this century. Language is a fundamental determinant of style. There never was one Lutheran culture right from the beginning.

Does a church still have to be established, financed and controlled by the state to be Lutheran? For obvious reason Lutherans in America made that basic shift in polity, although not necessarily in attitude.

The driving cultural question for today is whether leaders have to think theology and do church with assumptions that take member compliance and loyalty for granted, as could be done in an ethnic church body.

Can Lutherans move beyond intent to be the true church on earth to also being an effective church in social cultures that are mostly several generations past European ethnic roots?

The distinction between substance and style is really an invitation to discuss where, in this period of cultural change, the line can be drawn between what can change in church life and what cannot. What's inside the line remains unchangeable substance; what's outside the line is style that can change.

Surprising to me was the shape of exchanges at conferences that had formal presentations for and against openness to Evangelical style. Instead of rationally discussing what falls inside or outside the line to be faithfully

Lutheran, most vocal opponents took the emotional position that such a line could not be drawn at all. Everything Lutheran has to stay the way it is. Change the style and you change the theological substance. My question, "Even the sauerkraut suppers?" usually did not get an answer.

One exchange at a seminary exemplifies this attitude of rigid resistance to diversity of style. My dialogue partner was presenting the usual objection. One questioner from the floor noted that the earlier chapel service had been completely chanted. He did not have a singing voice. Was he somehow less Lutheran if he spoke it? My partner assured him that was okay. "See," I said, "you do agree with me; there can be a difference in style." The next week I received a letter from him faulting me for daring to suggest we agreed on this principle, which was unacceptable to him. That service, by the way, was completely chanted, without a homily or exposition of Scripture. I think our Lutheran ancestors would have found that to be a questionable change in public worship. The fact that seminary worship could omit a spoken message in itself demonstrates that worship is a matter of style for Lutherans. Style is what can change. Substance is what cannot.

One reviewer of the book thought a better distinction is the Aristotelian notion of substance as essence and accident as the outward manifestation of this essence. The outward manifestation has to be consistent with the essence. The substance "dogness" ceases to be a dog when it takes on attributes of a cat But one can readily recognize that dogness comes in dozens of breed manifestations that still remain dog, despite difference in tails, ears, legs, etc.

Can't there be dozens of manifestations of Lutheranism today that still remain Lutheran? Is there supposed to be only one expression of Missouri Synod Lutheranism that demands sameness in all details of church life, regardless of cultural setting and previous history of the participants? It remains hard for me to comprehend why a diversity of styles is not obviously acceptable. So where do you draw the line?

IS WORSHIP STYLE OR SUBSTANCE?

Should we declare our worship style to be substance? Such seems to be the interest of many who look longingly at the liturgically rich style of Eastern Orthodoxy. I learned some of the implications of that direction in discussion with a Russian Orthodox priest who heard about the book and wanted to explore applying some of the concepts to reviving church life and overcoming shallowness in his small declining parish. The discussion went nowhere. Changing style would be very difficult, especially for Sunday outreach, because the line for substance turns out to include the whole liturgy, which is basic to defining Orthodoxy. They have no equivalent of the Lutheran Confessions to spell out their unifying substance.

Part of that discussion highlighted how Orthodox parishes in this country are now typically small with very limited resources. This man's father had been a Russian Orthodox priest his whole working life; at retirement from his small parish he was earning the most salary ever, which was less than $20,000 a year. The reality for such specialized church culture is that few new residents looking for a church would think of checking out the local Greek or Russian Orthodox congregation. New members come by marriage, and there is not much point to community evangelism.

In an old city like Cleveland, Lutheranism is regarded by many residents as just one more ethnic church body like dozens of others. But Lutherans do not have to remain defined by inherited style. Our Lutheran Confessions spell out the substance and thereby give considerable freedom in practical application.

The Book of Concord is very explicit in declaring that worship is not a matter of substance. When stating a principle basic to Lutheranism the confessors used the very strong language "we believe, teach, and confess that...." What we know as public worship they discussed as "ceremonies, usages, and church rites."

The key confessional principle is presented in paragraph 9 of Article X of the Solid Declaration of the Formula of Concord of 1580:

> We further believe, teach, and confess that the community of God in every place and at every time has the right, authority, and power to change, to reduce, or to increase ceremonies according to its circumstances, as long as it does so without frivolity and offense but in an orderly and appropriate way, as at any time may seem to be most profitable, beneficial, and salutary for good order, Christian discipline, evangelical decorum, and the edification of the church. Paul instructs us how we can with a good conscience give in and yield to the weak in faith in such external matters of indifference. (underlining is mine)

The only other reference to public worship is in the earlier Augsburg Confession of 1530. In Article XXIV on the Mass, paragraph 1, the confessors say, "Our churches are falsely accused of abolishing the Mass. Actually, the Mass is retained among us and is celebrated with the greatest reverence."

The Mass is to be understood as the classic liturgy upon which the Divine Services of *Lutheran Worship* are modeled. Indeed, Luther's generation did continue to celebrate the classical mass—at least in Wittenberg. Reluctant to set an ideal pattern for other churches to follow, Luther entitled his basic service "An Order of Mass and Communion for the Church at Wittenberg."

Most significant for determining whether or not the Augsburg reference to the Mass is to be binding on other churches is the lack of the declaration "we believe, teach, and confess." The Augsburg statement is an observation offered particularly for political purposes. This Article XXIV ends with the summary appeal to the Emperor: Since we have made no conspicuous changes in the public ceremonies of the mass, it is unfair to criticize our worship as heretical or unchristian. Much more interested in personal relationships with God, Luther saw no reason to add confusion by changing anything more than necessary. External forms like worship were not nearly as important.

There is considerable evidence that Lutheran churches had a variety of worship formats a generation after Luther. Approving such variance was the central point of the Formula of Concord's principle that each congregation has the "right, authority, and power to change, to reduce, or to increase ceremonies."

For further discussion of the how Lutherans applied this principle over the centuries of their history, see my book *The Other Story of Lutherans at Worship*.[1]

CLOSED COMMUNION: SUBSTANCE OR STYLE?

In one heated conference the question arose: Is closed communion substance or style? I handled it poorly. Today I would say, Yes. The theology is substance. The way it is practiced is style.

This very tender topic makes a good illustration for line drawing. It also reflects the very different social environments faced by congregations within the same church body.

The apostolic theology is presented in 1 Corinthians 11: 27-29 with the clear statement that participants should be able to spiritually examine themselves for sin and repentance, and they should recognize that they receive the true body and blood of Christ in the bread and wine they are receiving. Furthermore, in view of 1 Corinthians 5:11, those who would commune but are living in public sin or have given public offense should first repent and seek to change this situation. The Lord's Supper is closed to those who are not baptized Christians and who do not meet the conditions set in these admonitions.

That's the *substance* of closed communion. The changeable *style* involves how decisions are made about who meets these conditions. One practice is for the pastor to be personally responsible for determining that each participant meets all the conditions. Another is to publicly declare the conditions and let the decision about meeting them rest with each interested participant. The first is the historic style, practiced in relatively small churches with few visitors. The second is the style emerging especially in large suburban churches with a constant flow of visitors.

As a child in my pastor father's parsonage, I remember taking telephone calls from members who wanted to *anmelden*, to announce for communion the next Sunday. That was the vestige of a traditional practice that in its best years brought pastor and individual parishioner together for a precious time of self examination and counseling. But those were years when communion was done only four times a year in congregations where the pastor could be expected to know everybody. It was also a time when pastors could be very paternalistic to members who were accustomed to doing what they were told was necessary to be a good Lutheran. A communion style that was once rich with opportunity for pastoral relationships lost its vitality by the time a quick telephone message left with a child could satisfy the condition.

Is the substance of closed communion changed when participants just fill out a registration card acknowledging their spiritual readiness to commune? Is it denied when they are referred to a written statement of the conditions without the expectation of a signed response? These are style issues of implementation, not substance.

Diversity of style does not mean that any communion practice is acceptable. Surely the conservative Lutheran theology of closing the Lord's Supper to Christians who do not recognize the Real Presence would be compromised by including a Christian who knowingly and publicly insists on symbolic presence. Then a pastor and congregation would be acknowledging their confession is not important. But that situation is not the same as admitting baptized believers who do not publicly confess an alternate belief or whose loose denominational affiliation does not represent their view. If the Lutheran conditions are stated, then the loving and pastoral application is to commune those who think they qualify.

Call this a practice of confessional communion that is ready to recognize individual faith. It assumes adults can determine for themselves whether they meet the conditions. To presuppose compliance until convinced otherwise does not have to compromise the theological substance. There is no inherent doctrinal reason to insist on the more cautious alternative that potential participants have it wrong until they publicly prove the right understanding. Interpreting charitably what your neighbor says and does is part of the Lutheran understanding of the eighth commandment.

In Lutheran tradition reason did at times exist prudently to withhold benefit of the doubt. If the king ordered your Lutheran village church to provide pastoral care for retired soldiers of strong Reformed beliefs, then admitting them to communion would compromise theological substance. This was the situation faced in Neuendettelsau, Bavaria, by Wilhelm Loehe, whose writings were very influential for the generation of leaders who founded the Lutheran Synod of Missouri, Ohio and other states. Many others of that generation formulated their practices out of reaction to a Prussian-mandated union between Lutheran and Reformed Churches that forced a compromise in theology of Real Presence. In a simpler world of well-known distinctions they were understandably resistant to a style that gave benefit of the doubt to visitors.

Discussing where to draw the line between substance and style can be especially productive regarding the condition of closing communion to those who are living in public offense or sin. This is the apostolic principle that Lutheran dogmaticians used in order to exclude any Christians who sin by following false teaching. False teaching in turn is defined as any denominational teachings different in the smallest detail from the church body with which the host congregation associates itself, even when the host Christians themselves are unaware of distinctions from previous centuries. A fundamental question begging to be asked is whether or not having doctrinal differences in slightest detail among confessing Christians really constitutes "living in public sin" for one side or the other. Is it necessary to also assume that an individual Christian knows and agrees with all the doctrinal subtleties of a church body with which he was once affiliated, especially if that church body does not have a precise confessional standard? Such an approach reads much more into denominational identities than exists in this country's church life today.

A communion practice that assumes the worst of an individual until proven otherwise seems a long way beyond what the Apostle Paul taught in 1 Corinthians. It unnecessarily excludes many fellow baptized Christians who do recognize the Real Presence and whose repentance is sincere and who are not living in commonly recognized public sin.

Much of the practice of closed communion is matters of changeable style. But not all. The growth of large metropolitan churches with transient participants provides good reason to reexamine the practice. Knowing where to draw the line is necessary to remain aggressively effective in settings where past debates and distinctions are for the most part forgotten.

---

1 David S. Luecke, *The Other Story of Lutherans at Worship: Reclaiming Our Heritage of Diversity*, Fellowship Ministries, 1995.

CHAPTER 4

Borrowing From Evangelicals
Or From Catholics?

Where should Lutheran church leaders look for concepts and advice on how to be and do church today? Scripture is, of course, the place to start. But where to look beyond the New Testament is increasingly at issue.

As American culture becomes more secular and transient, the challenges churches face today are in fact becoming more like those faced by the Apostles Paul and Peter. For some ways of doing church, this is good news. For others it is bad.

Attitude toward tradition makes much of the difference. The social disintegration in recent decades of American culture is bad news for church bodies that stay focused on church practices developed in clusters of centuries between the first and now. Their scholarship, significantly, looks back on that first century as the "primitive" church. Returning to first century social conditions is good news for churches that value returning to ways of the "early" churches. Many innovations and ideas that are fresh today were modeled in apostolic churches, such as informal worship, house churches, flexible organization and extensive lay leadership.

For most of their history Lutherans in America could look for ideas and take pointers by simply viewing what was happening in the old country. Except perhaps for a few specialties in German academic theology, those days are gone. The choice for reference point increasingly is between churches and leaders who, on the one hand, feature centuries between the first and now and those who, on the other hand, jump from the early church right to the practical challenges at hand. In Lutheran circles the first now surprisingly goes under the name catholic, with a small c. The alternative is one way to define Evangelical, with a big E.

Much of the heat and controversy around the book *Evangelical Style and Lutheran Substance* came from its positive regard toward American Evangelicals, in addition to its proposal to distinguish style from substance. Unlike most Lutheran lay people and the minority of pastors committed to church growth, most Lutheran professors and professional church leaders seem to operate with something like disdain for those who in America are now called Evangelicals.

EVANGELICAL

Much of the resistance has to do with different understandings of what amounts to a new use of the term on the religious scene of America. The word itself, of course, has long usage in German heritage, for it appears as one of the adjectives in the defining "Evangelical Lutheran Confessions." Today in this country it means, first of all, having a conservative theology and outlook, as opposed to mainline liberalism. Most movements in twentieth century church struggles revolved around trying to reinforce and thus distinguish conservative from the longer-established denominations "gone liberal." One of biggest of those movements was the "fundamentalism" that emerged in the early part of the century. Besides working with a highly literalist theology, fundamentalists were very separatist, and they splintered among themselves over the smallest difference in doctrinal detail.

Used in its root meaning of Gospel oriented and loving, the word "Evangelical" started emerging in the 1940s as the name of choice to distinguish conservatives who are less antagonistic, more outward oriented, and generally more appealing than the American Fundamentalists from which they took root. Today there are over 100 Christian denominations in America that do not feature their European heritage and thus are not mainline, Orthodox, or Roman Catholic. How do you write and talk about them as a group? Observers and national-level organizers have taken to the umbrella term "Evangelical" (usually with the capital E). The most doctrinaire and separatist conservative church groups, often Baptist, still prefer the term Fundamentalist.

What do Lutherans hear today when they encounter popular use of "Evangelical"?

Some hear "Fundamentalist" and think the discussion is about churches and people who used to operate on the lower-class fringes of American religious culture. The long drive of disciplined, upwardly mobile Lutherans was to become "mainline" and thus get beyond the ethnic fringes themselves. Few want to be associated with poorly educated fundamentalists. "Mainstream" is a better description of their longing. Ten years ago the initial suggestion for the adjective to put in front of substance in the title of the book was "mainline," as in Evangelical Style and Mainline Substance. I think the suggestion was meant in the sense of mainstream. Whatever else their agenda is, Lutherans today do not want to be marginalized anymore. Ironically, it is now the long-established "mainline" churches that have slipped to the margins of defining American church life.

34

Rejecting Arminianism

Many Lutherans today hear "Evangelical" and lump its many expressions together into one highly over-simplified category defined by them in such a way as to exemplify theology and practices most hostile to Lutheran substance. Some coarsely turn it into a whipping boy for all they focus on as wrong. And there are indeed expressions within the Evangelical camp that are simply unacceptable to Lutherans. Those expressions are conscious descendants of Arminianism, a well established theological term out of Reformed tradition that remains surprisingly unknown to most Lutheran theologians.

Named for a seventeenth century theologian, Arminianism describes understandings and practices that regard saving faith as partly a human effort and responsibility. Such faith can then easily slip into a kind of human work that becomes the basis for justification rather than relying on God's grace alone for confidence of a saving relationship with God. Then the believer can never be sure whether he or she has "enough" faith, and church life becomes a process of generating emotions that feel like faith and of insisting on behaviors that demonstrate faith. Martin Luther learned first hand the dangers of such an approach, and his descendants are rightfully ever on the alert against them.

So are many Evangelicals. The family of church bodies collected under the umbrella term "Evangelical" is big. Many who are now known as Evangelicals know how to spot and reject Arminianism as readily as Lutherans do. Lutheran critics of Evangelicals often complain about "Reformed tendencies" when they are really describing Arminian practices that many leaders from a Calvinist background would likewise oppose for the right reasons. But the issues go beyond unfamiliarity with a classic theological distinction.

The Inaccuracy Of Oversimplified Labels

American church life at the end of this century has been shaped by several tendencies that render unsound any theologizing by oversimplified labels. One is that Evangelical Christians take their Bible very seriously. The Holy Spirit is amazing in how he can lead readers, whatever their background, to the core of the Gospel—justification by grace through faith.

Another tendency is the widespread loss of regard for heritage. Many Evangelical churches and pastors today no longer match the description of the beliefs and practices associated with the formative years of their church body, which Lutherans may have learned through such guides as Lutheran F. E. Mayer's *The Religious Bodies of America*.[1] To condemn by denominational label may simply be inaccurate. It is certainly more difficult because of the rise of community churches without denominational claim.

A third tendency is for Evangelical pastors to be better educated than their predecessors. They are likely to be more conversant with broader issues of theology and more sensitive to subtle distinctions.

Vineyard Fellowships are pacesetters in church development in this decade. The association has expanded in twenty years from one congregation to now over 700—all by church planting. Predicting what one will encounter with a specific Vineyard fellowship and pastor is difficult. Some, like the revivalistic Airport Vineyard in Toronto, seem very strange, and this one was dropped from the Association. Other Vineyard pastors I have listened to and read seem very sensible, with good understandings of the Gospel and exciting ideas and track records for effective outreach. It should be possible, for instance, to promote stewardship evangelism, an approach modeled by a Vineyard pastor in Cincinnati, without being labeled and dismissed as supportive of revival excesses in Toronto.

So what is wrong with doing church in America today with oversimplified labels for others who are ministering effectively in the fields ripe for harvest? Nothing, for those who think their heritage gives them all they need to know to minister well today. A lot, for those who want to use their heritage as a foundation for building bridges to more effective ministry in American fields that are culturally quite different from what Lutheran predecessors faced. Some of the old ways no longer seem to be blessed as often by the Holy Spirit with a spirit of infectious growth. Some new ways pioneered by church leaders described as Evangelical are associated with such growth. Why let careless, ill-informed thinking limit Lutheran horizons?

The Promise Keepers movement is a good illustration. These conferences and follow-up small groups have had a strong Gospel impact on the lives of millions of men and families. God has richly blessed this innovative coalition of Evangelical leaders. Attitudes toward Promise Keepers can serve to differentiate Lutheran pastors and their mission orientation in some productive ways. Spot a Lutheran congregation that is openly supportive of Promise Keepers, and you probably have a Lutheran pastor more mission-minded than most of his colleagues. That congregation is also likely to worship differently from most others. I find nothing in the Promise Keepers' statement of faith that contradicts a Lutheran confession. Does support for the movement mean a pastor endorses every statement of every speaker? Who in today's society would jump to such a conclusion? I like the comment of a letter-to-the-editor writer who proposed to "eat the fish and spit out the bones." That is a good summary of how to approach Evangelical style for Lutherans.

CATHOLIC

For most Lutheran church professionals today, the alternative to Evangelical is catholic. Things "catholic" are very appealing, especially on seminary campuses. For the most part this word choice means things of the universal (catholic) church before the Reformation, of late seemingly extended beyond Roman Catholicism to include Eastern Orthodoxy. All this boils down to the historic liturgy and emphasis on the sacraments. The question of whether catholic worship can be separated from its Roman Catholic context does not seem to get asked. Nor does there seem to be much sensitivity to the dangers of "sacramentalism," the catholic excess opposite to Evangelical Arminianism.

A recent Lutheran seminary graduate pastoring locally has strong resistance to anything that can be associated with Evangelical. Partly this comes in reaction to Arminian excesses in his church experience before finding Lutheran theology. In his adamant insistence on using only the classic liturgy, he has proposed as a guiding principle the statement of the Lutheran Confessions regarding ceremonies and church usages, which are the historic terms for public worship. The principle is that "when a clearcut confession of faith is demanded of us, we dare not yield to the enemies in such indifferent things" (Formula of Concord, Epitome, Article X, paragraph 6). To him and many others the enemy are now Evangelicals. The only way is the catholic way. Therefore anything that smacks of worship in an Evangelical style of informality and contemporary song is to be rejected by true Lutherans.

My purpose for mentioning this exchange is to point out how much Lutheran heritage has been abandoned. That principle, enunciated in 1580, clearly and indisputably regarded the enemy as Roman Catholicism. For most of Lutheran history the appearance to be carefully avoided was Catholic.

Within living memory most Lutheran pastors wore simple black gowns. In the 1950s the black cassock robe with white overlay surplice became dominant, with the explanation that Martin Luther's generation of the sixteenth century continued to wear what they wore as Roman Catholic priests and what priests still wore. This appearance of catholic was acceptable because it was also Lutheran. But then the liturgical renewal movement in both these church bodies rediscovered the fourth century as a better reference point for fresh ideas. That is when Christianity first became publicly recognized and state-supported in the Roman Empire. This fourth-century change in status was accompanied by many new worship practices for assemblies that could now meet publicly in newly designed, special purpose church buildings. That was the century of the white alb gown with cincture and stole, which is now the formal vestment almost exclusively used among Lutherans. Lutherans can indeed change.

Disappearing Resistance
To Roman Catholic

Somewhere along the way resistance to appearing Roman Catholic disappeared. And then surprisingly the newest generation turned about-face to disavow any appearance as Evangelical. Now a seminarian can naively ask, as reported, "When did we lose the liturgy?" The truth is Lutheran church groups in America never had it in the sense he means until its appearance in recent decades. Some now want to turn into a mandate what first emerged widely in mid-century as an option.

Of course, the Lutheran substance of freedom in the Gospel prohibits turning any matter of style into a necessity. The companion principle to refusal to yield to the enemy in matters of indifference is the rejection of any effort to abolish freedom in matters that are neither commanded nor forbidden in Scripture (Formula of Concord, Solid Declaration, Article X, paragraph 30). Lutherans, of all Christians, should resist turning style into mandatory substance.

After dozens of debates and discussions, my overall conclusion is that the real issue for those Lutherans who want to be catholic is not historic ritual, or song, or vestments. It is the role of the sacraments in routine church life. Always important, Baptism and the Lord's Supper have become even more central to defining what being Lutheran means for institutional professionals developing Lutheran identity in seminaries and church body offices today. Much of their disdain for Evangelicals is that they are not sacramental in the same way. The core resistance is not to separating style from substance but to recognizing styles that challenge a newly emerging sacramentalism.

Theology of the nature and purpose of Baptism and the Lord's Supper are clearly Lutheran substance. But the frequency of reference to the

38

sacraments and their use in church life has indisputably changed. Because of this change, their use registers as a matter of style, even though the theology of the sacraments remains substance. There is a huge difference between church life that celebrates the Lord's Supper once every three months and life that revolves around worship centered on weekly observance. Defining that difference is the assignment of the later section on worship in chapter 9. In brief, the difference revolves around the importance of the preached Word. The danger is sacramentalism. To use the definition offered in the *Lutheran Cyclopedia*, this is "the tendency to give the Sacraments, specifically the Eucharist, a relatively higher inherent saving power than the Word. The tendency usually accompanies externalism in some form or another."[2]

What is the role of the preached Word in Lutheran congregations today? This is a key question about the basics of church life. A rough generalization is that pastors who give preaching high importance in attention and time tend to look more favorably on insights from Evangelical colleagues. Those for whom the preached Word has declined in preference to the Lord's Supper tend to look toward historic catholic precedents for their ideas.

---

1 F. E. Mayer's *The Religious Bodies of America*, Concordia Publishing House, 1954.
2 Erwin L. Lueker, Editor, *Lutheran Cyclopedia*, Concordia Publishing House, 1954, p. 935.

CHAPTER 5

Sociology Along With Theology

Working on my Master of Divinity thesis on church organization, my excitement was high at finding a new book by James Gustafson, a professor at the Divinity School of the University of Chicago. It was the first penetrating sociological study of the church that I had seen. It has become a classic. The title is *Treasure in Earthen Vessels*,[1] referring to 2 Corinthians 4:7. Its subtitle is *The Church As A Human Community*. Since then sociological studies of churches have proliferated and have been extended also back to what is known of New Testament times.

How easy it is for church leaders to forget that whenever the Gospel comes into contact with human beings it gets packaged in frail, breakable clay. This is especially true for the Gospel filtered through traditions and institutions. The treasure is the Gospel. Much of Lutheran tradition for conveying it remains earthen vessels, which is another way of saying style. Leaders who overlook the social realities of church life risk being blindsided when those human social realities change, as they inevitably do. To ignore the Christian church as also human communities is to invite irrelevance and ultimately unfaithfulness in carrying the treasure forward to those who need it today.

Part of the clash with Church Growth in the 1980s can be attributed to misunderstanding the difference between normative and descriptive statements. Lutherans do theology normatively, that is, by working out the way Christ's church *should be*, as established by Biblically based principles and norms. Sociology is a descriptive endeavor, offering observations on the dynamics of churches as they actually *are*, on human dynamics shared with other social communities. Anthropology is a close sister to sociology. Anthropology happens to be the doctoral discipline of several noted writers on Church Growth. My doctorate is in Organizational Behavior, which combines psychology and sociology to offer better understandings of human organizations.

The homogeneous unit principle recognized in Church Growth studies illustrates the different perspectives. It presents the observation that people like to go to church with others like themselves, similar in education, social class, and race. One has to look hard to find racially well integrated Christian congregations today—outside university cultures, where education and

41

social class are likely to be the common bond. According to Christian ethics, this is an awful principle to identify. Normatively it is wrong. Descriptively it is true much more often than not. Church planting or church growth strategies that refuse to recognize the reality of homogeneous social groupings will rarely be effective. This is not a nice message, but kicking out the sociological messenger is not going to change the social reality with which church leaders have to deal.

Acknowledging the all-too-human nature of real-life Christian congregations does not have to mean denial of the divine nature of God's church, any more than recognizing the human nature of Jesus does not have to mean denial of his divine nature. Jesus was both human and divine. So is his church. But his church continually has to struggle with the sinfulness of its human nature.

True, some sociologists do see only the human dimension of church, just like some theologians recognize only the human nature of Jesus. But many Christian sociologists as well as theologians stand ready to confess that God's own son Jesus is the source of a congregation's special identity as a fellowship, the body of Christ. In among all the too-human behaviors of a church, Bible-believing sociologists as well as theologians can recognize the Holy Spirit at work as he calls, gathers, enlightens, and sanctifies those people of God.

If there is any doubt whether I acknowledge dependence on the Holy Spirit for church growth, re-read the first section of the chapter on Regaining An Infectious Spirit (chapter 2).

VILLAGE CHURCH AND CAMP CHURCH

Evangelical Style and Lutheran Substance contained a sociological analysis of Lutheranism that has proved especially useful, as evidenced by references to it in the writings of others.

Lutheran styles of church and ministry were developed historically in the context of a village church at the center of a well-established community or parish. The new challenge facing Lutherans is to minister effectively in settings better described as a camp where participants are constantly coming and going. Summer camps were the formative experience for many American Evangelical church bodies.

For centuries well into the twentieth, most Lutherans lived on or near farms, as did most Europeans and Americans. Routine social life happened mostly in small villages that defined geographic parishes. Their religious life revolved around the parish church, which served generation after generation of the same families, for whom their land defined home. Church community was a given. Everybody knew everybody else in the area, and strangers were few. Members were literally born into the fellowship through infant baptism.

In contrast to village permanence is the temporariness of the camp church often seen on the frontier. People came together for a week or two and then went their own ways. Whatever was going to happen spiritually had to happen within days rather than over years. Community had to be built over and over again. Participants became used to talking about spiritual beliefs, and they found common bonds in identifying and telling their stories of being born again by the Spirit.

A village church typically does not have to worry about being effective in meeting felt needs or touching lives spiritually. Unless things really go sour, members will come anyhow, out of loyalty and in absence of an alternative. In contrast, effectiveness is basic to a camp church; otherwise participants will not return. Getting emotional is important in a camp setting, whereas strong emotions can be divisive in a village church and thus are avoided. In relationships of permanence, the Spirit is expected to come slowly. Where relationships are transient, the Spirit needs to come quickly.

The challenge for Lutheran ministry today is to develop new skills for post-village times. These are skills for building church community around spiritual experiences and commitments.

In a village, church conflict has to be avoided because members have no where else to go. The expectation that pastors have a university education usually meant having one from outside the village. This practice reduced the potential for conflict over leadership, since very few from within the village could aspire to higher education, which was very limited before this century.

The Lutheran state church structure that was organized around parishes helps explain the characteristic Lutheran topic of being the "true church." "True church" is not a Biblical phrase. "True" is, and also "church," but not the combination "true church." In the Reformation century of church conflict, the decision for what theological orientation would prevail in a region's village churches was made by the ruler of that region, and there were dozens of different political jurisdictions. Seeking and guaranteeing the ruler's approval led naturally to arguing that this confession was true and the others false. The opinions of village church members were of little relevance. The pastor's salary and continuance was dependent only on approval of the higher church authority accountable to the prince, duke, or elector.

Those social conditions are far distant from the American social setting today. It is time to add to "true church" more discussion also about "effective church".

DWELLING VS. SEEKING

An even newer sociological observation about churches today comes from Robert Wuthnow, professor of sociology at Princeton University. He is currently one of the best-respected interpreters of religious life in America. His book is *After Heaven: Spirituality in America Since the 1950s*.[2] The current situation is better described in the late 1990s, he suggests, by a distinction between a spirituality of dwelling and its contrast, a spirituality of seeking.

In his scheme the village church and the camp church would both be places where one can feel secure, be it a permanent dwelling or a temporary one. Both fit well in the religious boom of 1950s America, when reestablishing home was a dominant concern. Wuthnow observes, "People who enjoy the security of well-established homes and of enduring communities and who live orderly lives with familiar routines and organized roles can imagine that God is indeed in heaven and that the sacred may be worshiped within predefined spaces."[3] By the 1950s religious leaders had succeeded in rendering spirituality virtually equivalent to participating in a local congregation. At least three quarters of Americans belonged to a local house of worship. Clergy "worked hard to create the right kind of ambiance in morning worship services, increasingly through the full liturgical experience, including the mood set by the organ and by stained glass windows, and the accouterments of dress, carpeting, vaulted ceilings, welcoming foyers, and convenient parking."[4]

In contrast, the current time of accelerated social change leads to a spirituality of seeking and an emphasis on negotiation: Individuals search for sacred moments that reinforce their conviction that the divine exists, but these moments are fleeting; rather than knowing the territory, people explore new spiritual vistas, and they may have to negotiate among complex and confusing meanings of spirituality.[5] In seeker oriented spirituality, the congregation is less aptly characterized as a safe heaven. Rather it functions as a supplier of spiritual goods and services.[6]

Instead of the older pattern of institutional life with internalized rules and roles, the new pattern emphasizes looser connections, diversity, and negotiation; practical activity takes precedence over organizational positions. Rather than rules, symbolic messages prevail. In the past, places of worship were distinct buildings that drew people to leave the everyday world and enter a sacred space; now they are often nondescript, functional buildings that look like shopping malls and offices and that remind people of everyday life. Liturgy has shifted from providing a uniform experience to providing a highly variable one that encourages shopping and comparisons. Previously people participated as members of the church, expecting to live nearby and to contribute primarily to the support of the organization; now they are drawn by specific activities that they may support, such as a flower sale, the choir, or a marriage enrichment session.[7]

Normatively, this is a sad message. Accept it as a descriptive statement. Most church leaders can give examples of the increased difficulty of doing church in the ways of the 1950s. Most pastors of growing churches could provide illustrations of how different are the ways that seem to work today. The theological emphases and church practices of a well-settled village church are far distant from what many, but not all of today's seekers are likely to find helpful.

SO WHAT?

What to do with insights like these? The village/camp distinction first occurred to me when trying to explain to Lutheran college students why so many found attendance at neighboring Evangelical worship services to be more interesting and rewarding than what was going on in the traditional Lutheran services they were not attending anymore. Explanation helped them as well as their parents. Indeed, one of my clearest memories from the round of conference presentations following publication of the substance and style book is the number of pastors who would come up afterwards and share their ambivalent feelings. They were relieved their grown children were attending church, but confused and disappointed that they were doing this at Evangelical churches, not Lutheran.

Warning

Categories that explain are helpful. But sociological insights into religious behavior have greater value as a warning and a challenge. The warning is that being church always means applying spiritual truth to real people shaped by ongoing social dynamics. Practices that work well under one set of circumstances gradually lose their effectiveness when social settings change.

This is easiest to spot in the hundreds of dead and dying Lutheran churches in center-city areas where "our" kind of people left and other kinds moved in. There are still plenty of souls there in need of the Gospel, but traditional Lutheran ways of doing ministry too often seem to have little impact. What about the suburbs? Wuthnow describes changes in recent decades that are more subtle and more threatening because they apply as well to middle-class suburban settings where traditional Lutheran ways were doing well.

Not all Lutheran leaders need to heed this warning. Besides city churches and suburban churches, there are rural and small town Lutheran churches where village conditions still exist. In a recent random survey of Lutheran preachers that I did, over half described their setting as rural/ small town. Many of their churches may still be well-functioning healthy congregations. If so, keep on. Village style is a wonderful way of doing church that has served well over the centuries. Worshiping in German can be wonderful, too; it became problematic only when there were not many left who could handle the language. Village church style is a problem only when the sociological setting of relatively permanent residence, relationships, and commitments is withering away.

Challenge

Social change presents the challenge of church change. Then distinguishing style from substance becomes compelling in order to determine what can be done differently and what has to stay the same in order to remain faithfully Lutheran.

The changes proposed in the book ten years ago still seem many steps removed from altering doctrinal substance. They involve developing 1) better communication, especially in the major weekly event of worship, 2) fostering more personal faith expressions, 3) accepting informal, grassroots organizing, and 4) utilizing the full range of gifted leadership available among laity as well as clergy. Each of these proposals receives more extensive discussion in later chapters of this book.

The roots of resistance to these style proposals in Lutheran church bodies make update of the discussion important. Least worrisome is resistance to change in general. This is a fact of life in any organization and has to be expected in churches as well, be they Baptist, United Church of Christ, Lutheran or any other spiritual community of people who remain human.

Fostering change is the special responsibility of leaders. Thus more worrisome is the resistance of pastors. At least for the large proportion of those who are within a decade or so of retirement an attitude of just hanging on does seem understandable, as they count the remaining years with hope that the congregation stays healthy enough to maintain their salary in the meantime.

Thus more worrisome is the resistance of younger pastors who will shape the church of twenty years from now. A clear memory from the question and answer time of the many conference presentations I made is that the preponderance of young pastors who took the microphone to speak passionately for Lutheran tradition. In general I found more support among older pastors, who seem to have a better grasp of the issues.

Thus most worrisome is the resistance among the teachers of pastors, the seminary faculties. Things "catholic" seem to be of more interest. Few are the proponents of innovative mission, and they struggle to maintain voice. A worthy study would be a sociological analysis of how the two Missouri Synod seminary faculties became so narrow in their focus on tradition and conformity.

In recent years a very odd situation has developed. Practicing pastors are increasingly heading off in the direction of contemporary worship practices. The survey done in the summer of 1998 showed that twelve percent are doing "high" contemporary, a percentage that goes up to 43 when those doing "low" contemporary are added. Yet they are doing this without any guidance or training from the seminaries, where they encounter mostly derision for their effort. As any analyst of institutions will say, this is not a stable situation; something will change before long.

Who is out of step? Going back to the University of Wittenberg, Lutheran heritage is oriented towards having the pace set by faculty and their focus on truth. A reality of church life in America today is the withering of denominational influence; the vitality now rests with the local congregations, especially those that add effectiveness to concern about truth. It is inevitable that the growing churches will set the pace, unless they are forced out of the organization. In the Missouri Synod many of the largest have now established their own Pastoral Leadership Institute to better train ordained pastors to meet their needs.

The common denominator in this chapter is sociological analysis. To me the most perplexing part of resistance to change is the apparent denial by many church leaders that changed social settings will have an impact on ministry. They are willing to dismiss these trends by claiming that statistics can be made to say anything you want, so there is no need to pay attention.

A more rational position, though no more defensible, is enunciated by those who claim academic theology as their special contribution. They see everything a church does as deductions from theology. Thus nothing should change until theologians approve. Not surprisingly, they see little that is not substance.

Theologians unable to distinguish style from substance in church life risk "theological reductionism," a term used by James Gustafson to describe the faulty perspective that sees everything a church does as established only according to its divine nature. This is to be avoided as much as a sociological reductionism that sees only the human nature of a church. Churches in the grip of theological reductionism will have a hard time seeing beyond the traditions they have inherited.

One purpose of the first style and substance book and now this one is to challenge such a parochial, ill-informed posture. Theology expresses itself in church life, and church life expresses itself through real people who bring into their church life cultural patterns and conventions from the society around them. To ignore cultural changes in which ministry has to happen is to risk theological irrelevance.

---

1 James M Gustafson, *Treasure in Earthen Vessels: The Church as a Human Community*, University of Chicago Press, 1961.

2 Robert Wuthnow, *After Heaven: Spirituality in America Since the 1950s.* University of California Press, 1998.

3 Ibid, p. 7.

4 p. 30.

5 p. 4.

6 Robert Wuthnow, *Theology News and Notes*, Fuller Theological Seminary, Pasadena, California, March 1999, p. 5.

7 Wuthnow, *After Heaven, op. cit, p. 9.*

CHAPTER 6

Is Church Culture
A Means Or An End?

One hears talk among Lutherans of worship wars. Seldom used by the contemporary worship movement, the term comes mostly from defenders of the liturgical renewal movement of the previous generation. The conflict, though, is larger than worship. The division is really over assumptions about inherited church culture.

I join those who approach many Lutheran traditional practices as means to larger ministry ends. Others seem to imply that maintaining the culture of previous generations is an end in itself. Unlike the Synod conflict of 25 years ago, this one does not have basic doctrine at issue. The issue is inherited church culture—a means or an end.

Consider a simple example of a culture that is not churchly and thereby safer to discuss. Through my work with Chancellor William Danforth of Washington University in St. Louis, I was involved in the 1970s with a youth leadership development effort sponsored by the Danforth Foundation. The highlight was a two-week summer camp leadership conference at Camp Minnewanca in Michigan. The experience was highly programmed, using events, organizational structure, and vocabulary in place since almost the turn of the century. Each tent had an adult leader who had been doing this for ten, sometimes thirty, and even fifty years. These traditions worked well in producing the "Minnewanca magic" that had a strong positive, Christian impact on many teenagers.

That program no longer exists, however. Despite many dollars and much effort, enrollments declined. Times changed. The traditions had developed in the years before youth with leadership potential routinely went off to college. Through connections with the Ralston Purina Company many of those who came were from farms, and those demographics shifted. The biggest change was youth preference for summer camps with specialties, like basketball, cheer leading, soccer, horses, etc. Lutheran summer camps have struggled with this shift for years. The Camp Minnewanca traditions were good; this culture worked well—until it did not fit the times anymore. Then the Foundation needed to move on to other ways to make positive contributions.

Now consider the distinctive Lutheran culture developed around youth confirmation. Many of these traditions go back to village churches in communities where there was no high school, and the competition for social attention and effective teaching was minimal. It became a rite of passage that had much social significance in ethnic Lutheran communities.

What is the typical condition of Lutheran confirmation culture today? In congregations with enough children to offer classes, there is reason to believe the claim that "Kids hate it. Parents dread it. Pastors loathe it." Few programs claim much success for launching their kids into vital spiritual lives and active church involvement. Is there a better way to do it? Or does the tradition of weekly catechism instruction by the pastor need to be maintained to be a truly Lutheran church?

Cultural change usually comes through the contribution of a few innovators trying to do the job better. For Lutheran confirmation, Richard Melheim is one of those through his work with Faith Inkubators. Royal Redeemer has adopted some of his ideas. One is to add to the regular teaching time an opening worship with loud praise singing led by a teen band. Another is to shift the format every other week to small groups led by lay adults. This approach does not seem Lutheran. But kids ask to bring their friends. That does not seem to be Lutheran either. What an improvement in spiritual growth and evangelism! Do the kids memorize the blue catechism from cover to cover? No. Do they know enough doctrine to pass a big final written test? Yes. For all involved, this purposeful change in culture of a church is a worthy improvement.

EVANGELISM AND
A CULTURAL-LINGUISTIC TRADITION

Worship is inherently an expression of culture. The best formulated vision for the cause of liturgical advancement I have found was stated by Thomas Schattauer in his presentation to the Luther Seminary Convocation in January, 1996.[1] He is a liturgical scholar specializing in Wilhelm Loehe's work. Loehe studies, I am told, are hot now on Lutheran seminary campuses.

Schattauer presented the challenge of developing even further the culture of churchly life that makes the Christian church a distinctive culture. He proposes that such culture should form a wall separating through word, action, and sense the churchly life from all that is wrong with everyday culture. This calls for worship with "ritual and symbolic density," that recovers "dramatic density."

Dense walls? What would the building of dense churchly walls say about the mission of a church that pursues such a vision? Refuge from the world seems to be a greater concern than mission into the world. What evangelistic-minded pastor would want to put "ritual and symbolic density" in the way of unchurched and loosely churched seekers of an enriched relationship with God?

The clearest and best statement of differences on issues raised by *Evangelical Style and Lutheran Substance* was by Richard John Neuhaus in the August 1990 issue of *Lutheran Forum*.[2] He used the book to help illustrate what he thought is wrong with the Church Growth Movement. In many ways he serves as a spokesman for a catholic understanding of culture and ministry.

At one point he argues against evangelistic efforts to reduce a communication gap with those the church is trying to reach. He claims that "Christianity is a distinctive worldview, with a distinctive vocabulary, distinctive moral sensibilities, and a distinctive way of being in the world. It is...a cultural-linguistic tradition. One must be initiated into it, one must make a decision about it, one must cross the gap into another world."

Clearly in this understanding the cultural-linguistic tradition has become an end to itself. The primary goal is to maintain the traditions developed over the centuries and presumably then to apply them where possible. How different this approach is from seeing Christianity as all about relationships—redeemed relationships with Jesus Christ and changed relationships with each other. Rather than cultural, the basic gap to focus on should be spiritual. The world to cross over into is the one the Holy Spirit opens in the everyday life of those who hear Christ's call to follow him. Initiation should be into a relationship, not a culture.

For church leaders with catholic interests, these last few sentences will seem too "Evangelical." They fit the brand of Lutheran that I learned. "For me" was Luther's relationship language. To him everything revolved around Christ for me, not church for me.

Neuhaus had three other objections that express the heart of the issue very well. First and most forceful is his rejection of the proposition that the controlling purpose of the church is evangelism, defined, in his words, as marketing for the recruitment of members. The latter part of the statement needs comment. The first part, that evangelism should be the controlling purpose of the church, defines the issue. The rest of the discussion about style and church growth is shaped by position on that issue.

Only someone who does not value evangelism highly would define it as recruiting church members. That sort of language appears among writers in mainline and catholic church bodies and institutions. It is usually said in the context of declining budgets and the desire to have more members to maintain "the church."

To describe evangelism as recruitment already relegates it to the tail on the institutional church. As hard as it may be for Neuhaus and others in love with traditional culture to understand, there really are church leaders who regard evangelism as the controlling purpose of the church. From that perspective Christ remains the head, but sharing the Good News of who he is and what he does is the neck nerve cord that controls the rest of the body long before it ends at the tail. The best candidates for tail position are innovative practices from previous eras that once helped but are now ineffective. That such traditions should wag the dog just does not seem faithful ministry.

Two other self-formulated positions Neuhaus rejects are variations on the theme of church forms as dog or tail. He rejects seeing church as an enterprise whose product we are to design and market rather than as a community normatively shaped in time. Marketing shows up again a third time as a bad word in rejecting the view that the style or forms of a church's life are dispensable if that serves marketing goals. He states clearly his preference and that of many others with high loyalty to the catholic church of tradition. Evangelism should not displace practices established by the church of tradition as normative.

WHAT IS THE CHURCH'S PURPOSE?

Here is a way to rephrase the question. Should church forms and practices from centuries after the apostolic age be the controlling factor in shaping Gospel presentations today? Or should the Biblical, apostolic presentation of the Gospel reshape church forms and practices today? One's answer determines much about position on substance and style.

For me the answer depends basically on how one sees the purpose of the Gospel. It is supposed to have an impact that changes the lives of the people who receive it. This is the view of those who make evangelism the controlling purpose of the church. It was certainly the view of the early church. The other view—that tradition should the controlling factor—too easily loses focus on applying the Gospel to ordinary people where they are, in terms they can understand. This other view too often reaches out only to people who are willing and ready to fit themselves into the church culture at hand. This happens in many institutionalized churches that become controlled by human traditions.

That the Gospel should bring life-changing transformations is a good reason to think about marketing. While it is a bad word for traditionalists, this very contemporary concept, properly understood, can be helpful for those concerned about what kind of impact the Gospel is having on people here and now. It simply means letting those whose lives you are trying to impact help you figure out how to do that best by listening to them, instead of just presenting the Gospel in your favorite vocabulary and form—take it or leave it. The Apostle Paul took a marketing approach to his ministry when he was willing to become all things to all people so that he might save some of them by whatever means possible (1 Corinthians 9).

If traditions did not get in the way, there would be no need to import the non-traditional word "marketing." Then those shaped by the Gospel would find themselves naturally drawn to those who need it, and they would be finding out first-hand how best to communicate God's Word in ways that make a difference among those hearing it. Traditions freeze practices that once worked. But social cultures keep changing, as do the expectations of those who live in them and who need to find the Gospel difference. Feedback through a marketing attitude is one way to work at unfreezing institutions that are going out of touch.

Jesus did not need a marketing director. He was with the people he was trying to reach day in and day out, often literally in touch with their needs. The apostles did not need marketing specialists. They were of the people and in mission to them; they learned first hand how to minister so the Gospel made a difference.

In contrast, institutional churches loaded with tradition do need help from a marketing perspective in order to stay focused on their basic mission.

Is it possible that church leaders who read of declining numbers, like those descriptive of LCMS membership and attendance, react only in organizational terms? Apparently those who talk about recruitment do. I am among those who see attendance and membership numbers as a reflection of vitality, specifically spiritual vitality. Declining numbers reflect churches making a difference for fewer people and probably less of a difference for those few. This is a problem that goes beyond budgets. It gets to the heart of how the Gospel is understood and communicated. Declining numbers like those descriptive of the LCMS church body are a call to worry about churches drifting out of touch.

Many are the congregations and church bodies that got frozen into traditions which do not help the basic cause any more. But then getting hung up on traditions is a problem to worry about only for those who understand the cause as reaching out with the life-changing Gospel to people where they actually are rather than where they would have to be to fit into the church's existing culture.

But won't Lutheranism gradually lose special identity if its congregations look more like most of the other Evangelical churches out there? Perhaps. Undoubtedly style differences will become less apparent. Reputation for substantial focus on justification by grace through faith, though, should continue as strong as ever. That's what counts.

Again the question of purpose has to be asked. Is carrying forward quasi-Catholic traditions central to Lutheranism's mission today? Or is the purpose to be as effective as possible in carrying the Gospel forward to people who are not hearing it today?

Hear again Jesus' challenge that applies to congregations of disciples as well as to individual disciples: "If anyone would come after me, he must deny himself and take up his cross and follow me. For whoever wants to save his life will lose it, but whoever loses his life for me and for the gospel will save it."

---

1 Thomas Schattauer, "A Liturgical Prospect," his third presentation at the Luther Seminary Convocation in January 1996, St. Paul, Minnesota.
2 Richard John Neuhaus, "What's Really Wrong with the Church Growth Movement: The Lutheran Difference," *Lutheran Forum*, August 1990.

CHAPTER 7

The Strong And The Weak

Liturgical scholar Thomas Schattauer casts an instructive vision for what church life can be with a culture shaped with richly liturgical traditions. As highlighted in the previous chapter, he calls for worship with "ritual and symbolic density" that recovers "dramatic density." He does acknowledge one of the problems that the development of "density" creates, and this problem leads to the concern of the present chapter.[1]

Richly liturgical worship "presumes a lot." He notes that doing it well assumes a knowledge of the Bible, an active personal and family spiritual life, as well as ritual and musical capacities, all happening within a vital local church.

Church leaders on the front lines of congregational life know first-hand that these foundations are rapidly disappearing.

Sociologically, a church leadership vision that assumes so much for participation is properly described as elitist. Usually in discussions about worship styles someone enunciates the principle that we should be working to make Christians mature. The classic liturgy is mature worship. We should have mature worship for mature Christians. This seems reasonable and has certainly been persuasive for the many advocates of liturgical refinement. But it remains an elitist position.

About five years ago I began to put my finger on what feels wrong with this principle as a goal statement for ministry in most congregations. It overlooks the Apostle Paul's foundational teaching on the appropriate relationship between the weak and the strong in Christian community. One seldom hears or reads about the strong in relation to the weak anymore in Lutheran circles. I do remember it as a regular topic growing up in the Cleveland community of churches with the strong loyalties of ethnic Lutheranism. It had to do with warnings not to give offense to others in the community. Then it was hard for me to understand. Now in current application it is much more apparent. It has direct implications for the church mission.

Paul summarizes for the Corinthians this basic principle of apostolic style: "Be careful that the exercise of your freedom does not become a stumbling block to the weak" (1 Corinthians 8:9). There he was talking about eating food sacrificed to idols. The strong know that idols are nothing, and we are no worse if we eat food sacrificed to them or no better if we don't. But the weak may take offense at this freedom, which would then become a stumbling block to their continuance in the faith.

The proper theological term for what is involved here is adiaphora: Things neither commanded nor forbidden in Scripture. In Romans Paul develops the basic principle further. "Accept him whose faith is weak, without passing judgment on disputable matters" (14:1). The strong should not look down on the weak. Rather, "We who are strong ought to bear with the failings of the weak and not to please ourselves. Each of us should please his neighbor for his good, to build him up" (15:1, 2). The presenting issue is still food. Someone's faith allows him to eat everything, but another whose faith is weak eats only vegetables. The one who eats everything must not look down on him who does not.

STRENGTH AND WEAKNESS IN WORSHIP

Now in place of food, substitute style of singing or degree of structure in a worship service. These truly are matters of adiaphora. Some worshipers have refined their tastes to appreciate classic church music that meets high standards. Musically, they are more mature. Others find that a style of informality and of popular music with a beat helps them stay engaged. They could be dismissed as immature and told, directly or indirectly, to endure the higher quality until they finally appreciate it, until they grow up. A better term than immature to describe many is weak. A Biblical definition of weak comes shortly. For now consider the weak as beginners whose perspectives on the Christian life are just opening up—those to whom a congregation wants to reach out with evangelistic sensitivity.

Now hear Paul explain his apostolic approach: "Though I am free and belong to no man, I make myself a slave to everyone, to win as many as possible. To the Jews I became like a Jew, to win the Jews. To those under the law I became like one under the law so as to win those under the law. To those not having the law I became like one not having the law, so as to win those not having the law. To the weak I became weak, to win the weak. I have become all things to all men so that by all possible means I might save some. I do all this for the sake of the gospel, that I may share in its blessings" (1 Corinthians 9:19-23).

If the Apostle Paul were to enter the current debate between contemporary worship and classical liturgical worship, is there any doubt about the direction he would take?

What would Jesus do? What advise would he give to Lutheran churches today? We have a hint in his parable of the Pharisee and the Tax Collector. He was critical of the Pharisee who saw himself as the maturest of the mature, the strongest of the strong and who concentrated on doing everything right. Jesus had good things to say about the weak sinner who knew he needed mercy.

But, some may object, it is one thing to be considerate of the weak who are already in the church community; it is something else to extend the protection of the weak to include those unchurched who are not yet within. That stance poses interesting questions for ministry in generally middle-class America. If asked the question, "Are you a Christian?" by far most middle Americans would say "Yes." Nominal Christians would be the appropriate description for many of them. In communities like mine where Roman Catholic presence is unusually high, almost all report that they are baptized. In our experience at Royal Redeemer very seldom do we have an unbaptized adult among the unchurched we are reaching mostly through our contemporary worship.

In some formulations of Evangelical theology, having been baptized as an infant says nothing about whether such a person is a Christian now. But Lutheran baptismal theology should at least give pause before concluding that baptized, unchurched, nominal Christians do not qualify for inclusion among the community of weak Christians. Read again Paul's instruction as applied to weak, nominal Christians: We who are strong ought to bear with the failings of the weak and not to please ourselves. Each of us should please our neighbor for his good, to build him up.

The presenting issue for the tensions Paul faced then was insistence by some that certain foods were not appropriate for Christians to eat. One of the tensions among Lutherans today is insistence of some that certain forms of worship are not appropriate for Lutherans to do.

To this controversy over worship, apply now Paul's principles regarding the weak and the strong. The weak were those who insisted on a narrow view and thus missed the freedom in the Gospel that was basic to being a strong Christian. Could it be that the weak in the current issue are also those who insist on the narrow approach of only classic liturgy for proper Lutheran worship? They would certainly be surprised to be on the receiving end of the label weak, since mature worship for mature Christians is their agenda. But in apostolic style, maturity of knowledge and being strong in the Gospel are not the same. Such an application of Paul's principle would not be the first time the Gospel imperative reverses the normal order of things.

STYLES OF THINKING

Consider now a different approach to those who are looked down on as weak in church leadership circles. In years of teaching a Doctor of Ministry course on church management to over 200 practicing pastors, I developed a module on Styles of Thinking, using an INQ psychological profile.[2]

This questionnaire profile tested for five styles of thinking, called idealist, analyst, pragmatist, realist, synthesist. *Idealists*, among other things, typically seek ideal solutions, emphasize quality over quantity, try hard for perfect solutions, and screen out unpleasant data. *Analysts* seek the one best way, think prescriptively, and are best in structured and predictable situations. Very different are those whose dominant thinking style is *pragmatist*; they look for whatever works, are interested in innovation, are resourceful and flexible, and do best in complex situations that overload others. *Realists* point out realities and resources, focus on results, base decisions on facts and experience, and are good at simplifying. *Synthesists* see likeness in apparent unlikes, are curious and interested in change, focus on underlying assumptions, and stimulate debate.

The point of the exercise is to recognize the strengths and weaknesses of one's own dominant style, and then to learn to communicate better with those whose style of thinking is different. The Styles of Thinking profile is used most frequently for training sales people.

Idealist was the style of thinking usually dominant for about half the practicing Evangelical pastors in my classes. Many of these idealists also scored high on analyst. If anything, the proportion for Lutheran pastors is probably higher. The current tension over church culture in general and worship in particular becomes more understandable when recognizing that most Lutheran professional church leaders are idealists inclined to promote high standards, to emphasize quality over quantity, and to assume there is one best way. Historically this is what good Lutheranism does. Why settle for less than the best in church life, even if that means having to pull along a declining number of reluctant followers?

Pragmatists will point out what is wrong: "It doesn't work." Or at least it doesn't work as well as it used to. Missionaries tend to be pragmatists, looking for the shortest route to immediate pay off, identifying what will appeal to others, being open to innovation.

Which style of thinking is "strong," and which is "weak"? The answer is clear to idealists. To them pragmatists are sellouts who are too expedient, settle for trivial gains, and avoid long range planning.

But ask the pragmatists, and they will shake their heads about idealists who "can't get anything done" because they spend their time talking, planning, and trying too hard for the perfect solution. For instance, one group in a problem-solving exercise never got to the solution stage because they stayed stuck on the initial discussion of the problem they chose, which had something to do with alleviating poverty in South America. Later they all tested out as idealists.

It does not take great analytical ability to recognize that combining strengths makes a lot of sense. Having teams on which several styles of thinking are present can help overcome the weaknesses that accompany each. But team building does not seem to be a part of Lutheran heritage.

Recognizing different styles of thinking casts new light on the church growth controversies that were evident among LCMS pastors until forced underground in the mid-1990s. Almost by definition, church leaders who focus on numeric growth of congregations have a strong streak of pragmatism in them. Most church leaders who raise vocal opposition lean strongly toward idealism. That the two sides of the church growth debates would talk past each other is predictable. They think differently.

Good things could happen in the years when higher-level leadership forced the two approaches to stay in conversation. But when church growthers were "kicked off the team," the issues went into stalemate. In prolonged conflict between idealists and pragmatists in denominational affairs, it is not hard to project who will prevail in the long run, should the pragmatists choose to involve themselves in matters beyond the growth of their own congregations.

My personal style of thinking, by the way, tends toward a combination of synthesist and realist, which is what you could expect from an organizational psychologist (a realist) who writes a book trying to combine, or synthesize Evangelical style and Lutheran substance. According to statistics, this combination is present in 2% of the general population, infrequent enough to suggest "oddball" status.

---

1 Thomas Schattauer, "A Liturgical Prospect," his third presentation at the Luther Seminary Convocation in January 1996, St. Paul, Minnesota.

2 "INQ: Your Thinking Profile," Holland-Parlette Associationes, Educational Material, Inc., P.O. Box 10213, North Berkeley Station, Berkeley, California 94709-5213.

CHAPTER 8

Lutheran Substance

February 10, 1996, found me in the library of St. Matthew Lutheran Church in Walled Lake, Michigan. I was with two others: Judge Gene Schnelz, who was acting as the reconciler appointed by the Michigan District, and a pastor of that district with whom I had formally requested reconciliation according to synodical procedures for dispute resolution. This fellow minister had accused me of heresy in a review of my book *The Other Story of Lutherans at Worship* that had been run in a well-known newspaper favored by the hyper-orthodox.

The alleged heresy was teaching synergism. There were many other accusations, but they involved differing judgments about imprecise and emotive terms like "Reformed theology of glory," "pietism," "confusion of Law and Gospel." I think he used synergism likewise for its emotive value. But in Lutheran theology that term does have precise meaning, and I challenged him either to show how I was guilty of this heresy or to apologize. The outcome was a boxed off, written apology in the same newspaper.

Synergism means literally working together. While a good word in current business culture, it is a bad word for Lutherans when used to teach that a person can work together with the Holy Spirit on his or her own conversion. Lutherans condemn the view that in the will of the unregenerate there is a latent power for cooperating toward conversion. Such a view is carried forward in Arminian theology today. At issue is whether justification is by grace alone.

Justification by grace alone through faith alone is at the center of the Lutheran substance that must never be allowed to change. It is the defining characteristic of doing theology and church like a Lutheran. It is a position worth fighting for. Its companion principle is the freedom from legalism a Christian has in this Gospel truth.

One criticism of the book *Evangelical Style and Lutheran Substance* is that I said a lot about Evangelical style but almost nothing about Lutheran substance. This is fair. I thought I was writing a book for Lutherans about regaining an infectious spirit, and then the title was changed. My assumptions of common substance were left unexplored. This is a good time to clarify them.

61

Here are five beliefs that I think are basic to the Lutheranism I know and understand. There are more, but start with these:

1) the doctrine of the final authority of Scripture,

2) the real historical character of God's saving work recorded in Scripture,

3) eternal salvation only through personal trust in Christ,

4) the importance of evangelism and missions,

5) and the importance of a spiritually transformed life.

To say these are Lutheran is not to say Lutherans alone believe them. In fact, this particular listing and phrasing comes from a summary of common characteristics of American Evangelicals, as described by the leading historian of that movement, George Marsden.[1] This listing was in the book on style and substance, along with the observation that Missouri Synod Lutherans certainly have more in common with the holders of these beliefs than with branches of Lutheranism that would prefer to add extensive qualifications to all five.

From my experience of the last ten years, I now know that before affirming the fourth and fifth beliefs—the importance of evangelism and of a spiritually transformed life—there are many within the Missouri Synod who would want to state all sorts of qualifications.

I think the real issues of substance facing the LCMS revolve around the importance of evangelism and missions and the importance of a spiritually transformed life. I hope no leader in the Missouri Synod denies the theoretical importance of these core beliefs. But many do apparently keep these beliefs on the margins of their ministry.

ISSUES MORE BASIC THAN WORSHIP

Rather than argue about worship, would it not be more productive to stay focused on these more basic issues?

That very different understandings of the spiritually transformed life in Christ exist currently within the LCMS became more apparent to me in the dispute over synergism. Apparently there is teaching now that any human movement of Christians toward God is synergistic and bad, as evidenced in efforts to reject the singing of contemporary praise songs in public worship. It was my encouragement to do such singing that turned out to be the heresy my critic accused me of teaching.

I heard the same theme a year after the synergism conflict when I was representing contemporary worship in a dialogue for students on a Lutheran seminary campus. One student asked incredulously whether it is true that some Lutherans actually sing a song named "We Bring the Sacrifice of Praise." Yes, I said, it is one of my favorites. He clearly objected to the thought of bringing sacrifices in worship. He did not know what to say when I pointed out that the phrase came right from the Book of Hebrews (13:15), where a sacrifice of praise is seen as the fruit of lips that confess God's name. If this student had difficulty with the concept of sacrificial praise, how will he handle an invitation to sacrificial giving in congregational life?

This strange concept of worship without response comes from more than a student's or a pastor's misunderstanding. In a collection of essays published by the Commission on Worship of the LCMS, recognition is given to the dictionary definition of worship as a human activity going from the worshiper to the worshiped. Then comes this claim: "Such a view of worship is antithetical to the Evangelical Lutheran understanding of worship. The dictionary understanding makes worship our action or response.... The evangelical Lutheran understanding of worship is just the opposite. It is from God to us."[2] No wonder discussion of worship has become so difficult. Half the action has been disqualified at the outset.

If the dictionary has it wrong, how about the Biblical understanding of worship? The Greek *proskynein* is the most commonly used word translated as "worship" in the Old Testament Septuagint and in the New Testament. It means literally to bow before, which is a decidedly human action. Certainly Biblical worship begins with recognition of God's wonderful movement toward us, as proclaimed in his Word. But God expects a response. Should not worship planners, too?

Martin Luther's formative experience makes his followers especially sensitive to confusing the dynamics of justification with those of sanctification. The favor of God is not something we earn by what we do. There, synergism is wrong. But projecting the grace-centered, unearnable dynamics of justification onto the sanctified life of response does not do justice to Scriptural understandings of sanctification. There, "synergism," working with the Holy Spirit, is necessary. This simply means that Christians need to take personal responsibility for doing the things through which God can work out his will and his love in human lives, such as sharing Scripture, regularly praising God, purposefully serving their neighbor, and living a life that reflects a difference from their unsaved neighbors, however minimal.

Theologian Dietrich Bonhoeffer gave a well-known warning to Lutherans against treating God's forgiveness as cheap grace when they receive it as something that has no impact on the way they live. Is Luther's understanding of the sanctified life still being properly represented in teaching circles of synod?

Actually I question whether justification is also properly understood by many. I see this in fussing about the verb used to describe what happens when the promise of salvation becomes personal or is apprehended by the one coming to faith. Apprehension is the word used to define actualized faith (Latin: *fides actualis*), the technical term for that point in the classic order of salvation in scholastic Lutheran theology. Heaven forbid that a Lutheran would say, "I have decided to follow Jesus." In today's climate of oversimplified theology by label, "to decide" is an unacceptable Evangelical phrase.

But by dictionary definition, "to decide" is a wonderful word to describe what happens when the relationship with Jesus Christ as Savior becomes personal. By Latin etymology, the word means to cut off. Following Christ means cutting off reliance on other alternatives for taking direction in life. This is a great way to describe what happens. While justification by grace means no human on his or her own can decide to begin a redeemed relationship with Christ, those in whom God has established such a relationship certainly can and should decide to cut off alternative ways to believe and live. They "decide" to follow Christ.

For the last ten years I have carried in my wallet a slip of paper with a quote I looked forward to giving if opportunity arose. I could use it only twice. Here is a third time. It is a section from the second volume of Francis Pieper's *Christian Dogmatics*, which has been used to teach Lutheran doctrine to all Missouri Synod pastors since it was finished in 1920. His three volumes are as close as anything can come to the official doctrine of this church body.

In a section on saving faith, Pieper teaches: "Justifying faith is in every instance *fides actualis*, that is, the apprehension of the divine promises of the Gospel by an act of the intellect and will." Pieper then goes on to show that

> The Lutheran Confessions and Lutheran theologians declare that faith is
> an act not only of the intellect, but also of the will. They describe faith in
> such terms as desiring Christ, seeking Christ, demanding Him, as striving
> and running after Him, as stretching out the hands toward Him and em-
> bracing Him, approaching Him, running towards Him, as clinging to Christ
> and joining oneself to Him.[3]

It takes little stretch of the imagination to conclude that if Pieper and his predecessor dogmaticians had spoken English, he and they would have included "to decide for" in the long list of active verbs describing how *fides actualis* happens. Might Pieper even have had room for a phrase like "I gave my life to Jesus"? That is a good summary statement of what happens when Paul's exhortation in Romans 12:1-2 is taken seriously: "Offer your bodies as living sacrifices." What kind of theology does a Lutheran have who cannot endorse phrases like "accepting" or "receiving" the promise of salvation? Is it necessary to fault Lutherans who use a phrase similar to "I gave my life to Jesus"?

The hyper-orthodox tend to place high emphasis on the scholastic writings of seventeenth century Lutheran dogmaticians. Perhaps they should dig deeper into their sources for a truly Lutheran understanding of the role of actualized faith (*fides actualis*) in the order of salvation.

Ultimately it should be sufficient for me as a Lutheran pastor to declare that I wholeheartedly and enthusiastically subscribe *The Confessions of the Evangelical Lutheran Church*, for which my appreciation has grown over the years. I also wholeheartedly endorse the interpretations of Francis Pieper, for whom my appreciation has grown over the years. Any colleague in public ministry in the same church body should be given the respect of being considered fully Lutheran until proven otherwise. Should someone want to prove heretical theology, the proper way, the way of Matthew 18, is to begin with a direct one-on-one discussion.

The current tensions are not over doctrine. The issue is perspective on church culture, specifically how to shape church life and ministry in the broad range of practices that are neither commanded nor forbidden by Scripture. Here is where Lutherans should decisively lay claim to the freedom in the Gospel that is theirs in the pivotal teaching of justification by grace through faith. Issues of style dare not be legalistically turned into necessary substance.

LUTHERANS AND OTHER CHRISTIANS

Can one be a good Lutheran and still associate or even pray publicly with Christians of different church bodies? This is the best I can phrase the issue that for many seems to test allegiance to Lutheran substance. Incredibly, I write this with fresh memory of official reprimand given to two Missouri Synod district presidents for participation in church-like public events with other Christians, one at a wedding for a relative and the other at a community rally of religious leaders promoting street safety.

Another angle on the same general issue presents itself with denominational displeasure expressed toward Lutherans who involve themselves with Evangelical para-church organizations, like Promise Keepers. Nineteenth-century theological phrases like "unionism," "fellowship," and "heterodox" beg for clarification.

A thoughtful distinction between substance and style can help Lutheran church leaders remain faithful while pursuing aggressive mission amid the realities of twenty-first century church life in America. Faithful membership in the "whole Christian church on earth" calls for living in creative tension with brothers and sisters of the Christian faith even when they depart from distinctive understandings of our Lutheran confession.

Of substance is the importance of not compromising the teaching of doctrinal positions officially held by the Lutheran church body in which one holds membership. One could not subscribe the Reformed Westminster Confession and still expect to be taken seriously as a Lutheran. On a continuum of potential compromise there is a huge difference, at the one extreme, between subscribing a contradictory confession and, on the other extreme, simply praying together, publicly or privately, with a pastor of a different church body. Making distinctions on the continuum has to do with appearances. And what constitutes the appearance of compromise is really a matter determined more accurately by social convention than by a theological dictum frozen in the cultural conventions of a previous time. The social interpretation of church practices and customs is determined, to a large extent, by the social conventions of the day. That is why they are matters of changeable style.

Who in today's America would conclude that a Lutheran church professional appearing in the vestments of his calling with a similarly vested Roman Catholic archbishop at a public community event is compromising his doctrinal confession? Or who would propose today that a pastor participating the wedding of a relative in the church of a different Lutheran denomination no longer cares about his distinctive Lutheran beliefs?

In answering a questionnaire, would any observers conclude that either church official must not be a good Lutheran? How strange an observer with such a view would appear among other church people, let alone to secular spectators. Does anyone seriously think that representatives of one Christian denomination who refrain from participating with a hundred others in a public event would somehow show up all the others to be false? If anyone noticed, would such absence leave a Gospel-affirming impression? Social appearances change over time. What may have looked like a unionistic practice 150 years ago in Germany no longer appears so in America today. That does not mean the substance of confessional integrity has changed.

Because of their history, Missouri Synod Lutherans carry a tradition laden with foreboding about association with heterodox congregations or missionary activities. The concept of heterodox, or teaching falsely, lends itself again to constructive distinction between substance and style.

"Heterodox" is the opposite of orthodox. It is meant to describe church bodies or agencies that present false doctrine. How does one determine whether a church or para-church organization is heterodox? Is it so if anyone involved in it anywhere departs in any way from any teaching of the orthodox church body? Or is that status reserved for bodies or agencies that expect formal allegiance to a statement of beliefs that contains false teaching? What if that organization has no formal statements of beliefs at all, a situation increasingly common in church life today?

The substance is confessional integrity. The style is how much formality one looks for and how narrow or how broad an interpretation one uses to determine whether a specific group of Christians is heterodox.

I offer as an example my relation to Fuller Theological Seminary in Pasadena, California. It is an interdenominational school with representation from some 70 different church-body heritages. I was one of the few Lutherans. Fuller has a carefully formulated Statement of Beliefs. In fact, as vice president I was charged with assuring subscription on the part of staff and students. Were the statements exactly the way a confessional Lutheran would formulate them? Mostly, but not exactly. For instance, the statement affirmed the importance of word and sacrament ministry. But it did not go on to define baptism and Lord's Supper, let alone to profess Real Presence. The statement on sacraments was purposely short and general. Indeed all possible understandings of communion were represented among faculty. In affirming this statement of the importance of word and sacrament ministry, was I endorsing a Zwinglian or a Calvinist interpretation? How could such an interpretation be made when all I agreed to is that the sacraments are important?

After careful study, I confidently concluded that subscribing the formal one-page Fuller Seminary Statement of Beliefs did not compromise my subscription to the historic Confessions of the Evangelical Lutheran Church. Other Lutherans may disagree. I propose we are in the realm of differing style for expressing the same substance of confessional integrity.

I have found it helpful to discuss the relation of LCMS leaders and congregations with other Christians in the context of two circles.

Fellowship with those in total agreement.

Cooperative relationships with Christian agencies or groups which have no formal confession, or whose confession does not contradict Lutheran doctrine.

No formal relationships with churches whose official confession denies Lutheran doctorine

Inside the inner circle represents ministry relationships only with those in full agreement on all teachings of the church body. There is the LCMS approach to the highest level of fellowship—formal pulpit and altar recognition. Does it also have to be standard for all other forms of cooperative relationship?

Outside the outer circle are Christians whose formal confession contradicts Lutheran substance. These typically would be Christians in denominations that have a formal confession that the members are aware of. The space between the inner and outer circles represents Christian individuals, agencies or groups which have no formal confession, or whose confession does not contradict Lutheran doctrine.

One can do church and ministry by dealing only with leaders and churches that are inside the inside circle; that is, they are in full formal agreement on everything. This is safe. This is the Missouri Synod heritage. But this approach is more appropriate to a time when denominational loyalties and differences were known and when few parachurch organizations were active across denominations.

Such avoidance, though, eliminates many opportunities for effective ministry through leaders, programs, and agencies that are clearly advancing the kingdom of God in exciting ways acceptable to mission-minded Lutherans. The obvious example is Promise Keepers, which does have a formal, four-paragraph statement of beliefs. I challenge others to find statements in it that contradict Lutheran understandings. On the other hand, I could not support an agency or school that requires endorsement of a formal confession that falsifies Lutheran beliefs.

The traditional LCMS approach views others as heterodox when they are not in full agreement on all details of a church body's confession. That is a very narrow definition that may have fit the times of the nineteenth century. Does that traditional interpretation have to extend now to ministry in the twenty-first century?

The reasons to challenge this tradition are a) to pursue greater effectiveness in mission fields of today, both at home and abroad, and b) to reach out to fellow Christians as far as possible without compromising confessional integrity. The broader definition of heterodox eliminates only those whose formal confession contradicts Lutheran teachings. Somewhere between inside the small circle and outside the large circle are a great many Christians who offer opportunities for ministries that Lutheran congregations can learn from and support on the way to more effectively touching lives with the Gospel.

---

1 George Marsden, *Evangelicalism and Modern America*, Eerdmans, 1984, pp. ix.

2 Roger D. Pittelko, "Corporate Worship of the Church," *Lutheran Worship: History and Practice*, ed Fred L. Precht, CPH, 1993, p. 45.

3 Francis Pieper, "Saving Faith as '*Fides Actualis*'", *Christian Dogmatics*, Vol II, Concordia Publishing House, 1951, pp. 432-433.

PART II

Better Ways To Communicate And Organize

CHAPTER 9

Better Communication
In Worship

The congregation I was visiting seemed to pulsate with life and with excitement for ministering to others. Christ Church in Tver, Russia, in 1995 was a new church with almost no remembered heritage. Despite the setting of a dimly lit theater, it was bright with hope and anticipation.

The collapse of communism brought new spiritual possibilities to people looking for purpose in this run-down city 90 miles north of Moscow. In this congregation the longest anyone had been a Christian was three years. The congregation started with a woman who brought new knowledge and conviction of the Gospel back from a crusade in Moscow. Her husband soon became a believer, and their infectious spirit spread rapidly into a congregation worshiping about 300. She was the evangelist; he became the pastor. They figured out what to do as they went along. Having never seen a Christian church wedding, they made one up when the need arose.

In their openness to Christianity, many of the new believers I talked to in that church had tried out Russian Orthodox services. These left them cold; they found little that engaged them. Orthodoxy was reasserting its religious claim, but it was doing so through collaboration with state powers, not through evangelistic appeals.

There were two styles of communication going on in these different kinds of worship service. In one the intent was to appeal as directly as possible to people who were seeking a new faith and all it had to offer. Everything was very simple. The one common denominator was a well-marked Bible most had in hand. The half hour of singing could be done without words printed on paper or projected overhead. In my message I was expected to call for a response. The service ended with various small groupings of participants praying together.

The style of communication in this worship setting was oriented toward drawing people into heartfelt relationship through singing, a more informed relationship through direct scriptural teaching, and closer relationships with each other through praying. How could anyone come away without admiration for what the Holy Spirit had accomplished there in such short time?

While I personally did not have opportunity to participate in the Orthodox alternative in Tver, I can guess what new Christians encountered. The richly liturgical worship would communicate by rituals and symbols that the event was for people who already knew a lot about Christianity. Relationships with God and others would stay impersonal through scripted words and symbols. Those who had tried an Orthodox service reported their feelings of discomfort and distance from others rather than joy of being personally welcomed into an exciting group of Christians.

Encountering traditions about relationships is not the same as experiencing relationships. Styles of communication in worship differ in what they try to accomplish. Worship that features traditions from previous centuries may well engage the minds and hearts of some participants. But how many? What about the others? The basic problem arises when a worship style is used with little concern about what happens to those in attendance, especially the new ones. What are officients in such worship trying to accomplish? Staying fixated on a style that communicates ineffectively with many participants seems fundamentally foolish. Does not good and faithful churchmanship call for accepting the challenge to improve the communication going on in worship as well as in other parts of a church's offerings?

Being ready to change traditions for the sake of more effective communication in worship is now known as doing "contemporary worship." Perhaps a name that could be as descriptive is "informal worship." In this generation of Lutherans the featured tradition being left behind is the classic liturgy with its layers of meaning and symbolism. One reason contemporary, informal worship is spreading so quickly among Lutheran churches is simply that these services communicate with those gathered better than the alternative. For a description of such services, see my book *The Other Story of Lutherans at Worship.* [1]

To communicate better means to be more effective at sending messages that bring an intended response from others. If there is little response, then the music and words were not very effective at shaping the worship of a gathering of Christians. The ultimate "no response" is absence from further gatherings. That traditional Lutheran worship communication is losing effectiveness is a basic meaning of the decline of average worship attendance from 173 to 155 in the last ten years among congregations in the Lutheran Church—Missouri Synod.

How important is it to have better communication of Lutheran substance in worship? The answer depends on how much importance is at-

74

tached to having continued vitality of Lutheran congregations into the next generations.

APOSTOLIC WORSHIP

How did the Christians of apostolic times worship?

A starting point is to recognize that they did not all worship the same way.

The earliest Christians were Jewish, and they undoubtedly continued their synagogue traditions. But soon the Apostle Paul took the Gospel to Gentiles. He chose to spend a lot of time and effort preventing the Judaizers from imposing their traditions on Christians who knew nothing of Jewish ways. As Apostle James declared, "We should not make it difficult for the Gentiles who are turning to God." Casting off traditions was basic to the Gospel freedom Paul proclaimed.

The Jewish Christians who spoke Greek may have talked about their worship as "liturgy," the word used for their ceremonies in the Greek translation of the Hebrew Old Testament. But the word "liturgy" is used in the New Testament in a similar sense only in the Book of Hebrews, where the consistent meaning is that the former rituals and priestly roles have all been fulfilled in Christ and are no longer relevant to Christians.[2]

An Orthodox priest once explained to me that their liturgy continues the form of worship directly instituted by God, which therefore is more pleasing to him. That could be true only if the new era clarified in the Book to the Hebrews were left out of the discussion.

So how did Gentile Christians worship? Apparently worship forms were not important enough to write about since little is said in the rest of the New Testament. In Acts 2 we have a glimpse of what the brand-new Christians did together right after Pentecost. They became a fellowship or partnership of believers who pooled their possessions, ate meals together, listened to teachings by the apostles, and prayed.

How much the breaking of bread refers to the special remembrance of Jesus in bread and wine is unclear. The major point, emphasized in verse 46, is that they shared meals. It would have been natural in the course of such meals to include remembrance of how Jesus offered bread and wine as his body and blood. There is no indication that they celebrated the Lord's Supper at any time other than as part of a regular meal they were sharing. And sharing everyday food remained a high priority, as indicated in the appointment of food administrators in Acts 6.

The second glimpse of worship appears in Paul's first letter to the Corinthians, chapter 11. These believers, too, shared meals. This component becomes all the more understandable with the realization that they met in someone's house, for there were no special church buildings beyond the synagogue. Over the years, though, the quality of fellowship deteriorated, so that some who brought little went hungry while others who brought much got drunk. Paul's main point is that such unloving behavior did not fit with the remembrance of Jesus that they celebrated as part of their time together. The solution was not to separate the Lord's Supper as a ceremony apart from the regular meal. It was to be better behaved and more considerate at the regular supper: "When you come together to eat, wait for each other."

The other glimpse comes a few chapters later. In chapter 14 Paul emphasizes what we would call ministry of the Word. It was carried out with vigor that was very engaging. "Everyone has a hymn, or a word of instruction, a revelation, a tongue, or an interpretation." The Word was shared with such exuberance and high spirits that Paul was concerned about maintaining some sensible structure. But improvement did not come through imposing a rigid order, for he says, "If a revelation comes to someone who is sitting down, the first speaker should stop." He expected spontaneity. Just be more polite and take turns, he tells them. All the words spoken must be done for the strengthening of the church

What little we can know about apostolic Gentile worship suggests something that is very different from what we have today: an inflexible structure of scripted words that are repeated in the same order week after week, with only one person giving a short ten or fifteen-minute homily and then presiding over a distribution of wafers and wine separated completely from a shared meal of regular food. The sharing that Paul's congregations did must have taken hours. The modern service of 55 minutes from beginning to dismissal would probably be very suspect to them.

LITURGY INCREASING,
PREACHING DECREASING

"As the liturgy increased, so preaching decreased."

This the observation of Lutheran professor of preaching, Gracia Grindal, who continues, "Our decline as Lutheran churches can be directly linked to the decline of preaching and the abandonment of the simple liturgies bequeathed us by Luther, and used by all of our predecessor bodies."[3]

Is preaching really declining? Consider what is happening to length of sermon and priority of preaching.

Two out of three Lutheran preachers aim for a sermon of less than fifteen minutes. Younger preachers (10 years or less experience) are more inclined to do short sermons—80% compared to 60% of their colleagues whose seminary days are farther behind.

Only about three out of ten Lutheran pastors regard the sermon as the most important part of the service. Again, the younger ones are even less so inclined—24% compared to 32% for the rest.

The numbers suggest that a trend toward de-emphasis of the preached Word in Lutheran worship continues right now.

How would such statistics turn out for Lutheran pastors a hundred years ago? Written sermons from that era suggest a normal delivery length of half an hour to 45 minutes. There was no competition to the sermon, since communion was usually celebrated only quarterly. These pastors would say obviously the sermon is the most important part. In fact, in German the usual name for their position was the *Predigtamt*, the preaching office.

The statistics for current ministry come from survey research I did in the summer of 1998 for an article on preaching trends in the journal *Word and World*.[4] It reported results of a questionnaire completed by 169 Lutheran pastors selected at random from the rosters of the LCMS and ELCA in roughly the same proportion as their total numbers.

But a counter-trend toward better communication is developing. This is an observation from the same survey done separately among a specially selected grouping of pastors recognized as trendsetters in doing contemporary worship.

These pastors place much more emphasis on preaching. Instead of only one third of the random sample, two thirds of the trendsetters aimed for a sermon longer than fifteen minutes. Two thirds regarded the sermon as the most important part of the service, compared to only 30% of the general sample.

These pastors were also three and a half times more likely to report significant growth in attendance. They were selected because they do contemporary worship. In the larger sample all those who reported any kind of contemporary worship were two thirds again more likely to report growth in attendance than those who did not.

The outcome of this comparison of growth rate was predicted in *Evangelical Style and Lutheran Substance* ten years ago. There, the first of four concluding chapters on style highlighted the importance of gaining and maintaining audience contact. This is harder to accomplish when everything is scripted and routinely predictable. It happens through preaching that takes the time to be personal, to tell stories, to make analogies and to anticipate responsiveness.

Better audience contact also happens with topical preaching that more directly addresses concerns of the listeners. Lectionary preaching, based on predetermined texts for that Sunday, is clearly the norm among Lutherans. In the random sample, this is identified as the most characteristic approach by 87% of the respondents. In comparison, only 32% of the trendsetters depend on the lectionary; 68% describe topical preaching as their most characteristic approach. Also, trendsetters were half again as likely to agree that the needs and interests of the hearers should be the primary concern in preaching.

Audience-oriented, longer, topical preaching is associated with the church growth. This outcome fits the overall thesis of the earlier book that infectious growth was more likely among churches that have the four style characteristics recommended in this and the next three chapters. I hasten to repeat that these styles by themselves do not bring growth; that is the work of the Holy Spirit. But where the Spirit grants unusual growth, the styles of communicating and organizing tend to be different from the norm.

To focus on audience contact itself is controversial. The liturgical preference is to see everyone as participants, which is laudable. But this assumption often results in taking the audience for granted, and thus leaves many behind. The concept of audience was not foreign to our predecessors. Theirs was a preaching service. This mindset could build a Clayton campus for Concordia Seminary that for forty years had only an "auditorium," which was deemed sufficient.

The Apostle Paul knew about audience contact. He shifted from Hebrew to Greek to Aramaic depending on which communicated best to those he was trying to reach. He continually worked hard to get a hearing from the disinterested as well as those who were opposed to his message.

Gracia Grindal notes how Martin Luther in his pamphlet "Concerning the Ministry" hammers on the notion that preaching is the first office of the pastor, "Inasmuch as the office of preaching the Gospel is the greatest of all and certainly apostolic, it becomes the foundation for all other functions." Luther notes how Christ did not baptize, but proclaimed the Gospel, and Paul gloried in the fact that he was sent not to baptize but to preach. Even the Evangelists and Apostles, according to Luther seldom, "make mention of the Eucharist, a fact that has led many to wish they had said more about it. On the other hand, they ceaselessly emphasize, to the point of weariness, the ministry of the Word."[5]

THE COMMUNICATION
VALUE OF REPETITION

The ministry of the Word can be done with differing styles in a worship service. Classic liturgical formats use phrases, statements and responses that are for the most part literally the Word of God. Is there a difference between reliance upon presenting the Word, on the hand, in predictable, predetermined liturgical passages that stay mostly the same from week to week, or reliance, on the other hand, upon presenting the Word in preached format that is intended to bring fresh perspective on differing portions of Scripture. The difference emerges in attitude toward the communication value of repetition. Is repetition a help or a hindrance in accomplishing what God's Word is supposed to do?

Repetition is helpful for those whose intent is to imprint God's claims and promises deeply on the consciousness of those assembled for worship. Repetition is the key, one often hears among advocates of more liturgical worship. Recreate the same drama in the same words weekly, and God's Word will became the framework for interpreting the rest of life. Enrich religious life with constantly used symbols that will remind individuals of what life with God should be.

In this approach improvement in religious communication comes by adding symbols in layers of reminders of the same basic actions and responses; repetitive density in communication is good. It adds depth for those who know what they mean. Teaching symbols becomes important because they can convey meaning only for participants who already know them. Reduce the number and frequency of symbols in use, and worship becomes dumbed down and even trivialized. Life with God is enriched through worship with an abundance of predictable symbols.

That is one approach. Rather than a help, repetition can also be seen as a hindrance, something to be overcome. This happens with a different understanding of communication. Instead of trying to reinforce existing understandings, the goal of this other approach is to have an "impact," to make a difference in how recipients perceive and understand something. One of the basics of information theory is that the amount of "information," or impact, carried by any item is directly proportionate to its unpredictability. If the occurrence of a particular word or expression can

79

be predicted, then the word has little impact; it does not engage attentiveness or thoughts.

Eugene Nida was a specialist in communicating the Christian faith. He oversaw translation for the American Bible Society and was especially attentive to the linguistic challenges faced by missionaries. In his discussion of information theory he points out that every message must have some predictability or redundance, lest the hearer is overloaded with specialized words or expessions that convey no meaning to him and thus have little impact. The challenge is the right mixture. Too many unpredictable words with specialized meaning leave the listener lost. Too little unpredictability "runs the opposite risk of producing nothing but a series of trite, warmed-over expressions which may flow out in incredible monotony and sound exceedingly pious. Here the 'informational' content is exceedingly low."[6]

Another principle is that the greater the specificity of detail the greater is the information. An account of specific events is much less predictable than generalized observations. This is why people get more out of new illustrations than from familiar generalizations. Nida points out that Jesus was the master communicator because he not only spoke the simple language of the people but also framed his teachings in forms—such as parables—that have optimum "informational value" as well as truth. His words were truth with impact.[7]

Although Jesus knew well the repetitive ritual phrases and passages of the synagogue, he made little use of them is his communication. Rather he specialized in stories and parable illustrations with personal application. Why did Jesus choose to go for fresh impact rather than for repetitive reinforcement?

At issue is what communication of the Christian faith is supposed to accomplish. Jesus was all about extending the kingdom of God farther into the lives of individuals and communities. He wanted God's reign to have stronger hold on the lives of his people. Jesus communicated for the purpose of changing people. He went for impact.

What is the purpose of the communication that happens in the Sunday morning hour or so of a worship service? Is it to *reinforce* God's hold on his people? Or is it to *expand* his hold on those who regularly gather? Or is it to *extend* his reach out to those on whom God's kingdom has had little impact yet? The intended outcome will shape the style of communication that is featured.

The repetitive, predictable phrases and sequences of the classic liturgy work well for *reinforcing* God's hold on those who already know what life with him should be all about and just need to be reminded. The more reminders in words and symbols, the more effective the worship experience will be for the intended participants.

If the purpose is to *expand* God's kingdom within the lives of his people, then the communication needs to convey more "information." It needs to have more impact. For this purpose repetition is of little help in bringing about the changes and the "newness" that God's Word is supposed to accomplish.

If the purpose is to *extend* God's kingdom to those who do not yet know him well, then liturgical repetition is actually a hindrance, because it presents specialized language and symbols that can have little meaning to the uninitiated. For the initiated, the repetition can become boring because the meaning is predictable. For the newcomer, the repetition can become boring because the meanings are not yet known and the incentive to learn them is not yet strong.

Jesus' mission was to change people. That is why he communicated for impact. His churches differ in their commitment to that mission. Those that give priority to the mission of changing people inevitably place greater emphasis on communicating for impact, presenting fresh perspectives that call for new or renewed responses to God's claims. This is the task of ministry of the Word, especially as the Word of God is applied and made relevant to the needs and expectations of the hearers at hand. This historically is the function of the sermon. The greater the intent to change people with God's Word, the more the sermon rises in importance in the worship services of churches.

How to make the sermon more effective at its intended purpose is a separate issue for discussion somewhere else. The point here is simply that in churches where the amount of time given to preaching has shrunk from half an hour down to ten minutes in preference to liturgical enrichment, something significant has happened to their basic mission. It is not a direction that leads to greater vitality, new energy, and more effective outreach.

One opinion that became fashionable in the 1960s was that monologue preaching as a form of communication had little future because of the increased competition from movies and TV that were more effective at gaining and holding attention. Like the fashionable prediction that Christianity was on its last legs in the West, this one about the declining effectiveness of single-person speaking has simply not come about. The best evidence can be seen motivational seminars that regularly tour cities and charge high prices for the experience of sitting in a large auditorium for a whole day and listening to 45-minute speeches by one talented speaker after another, usually without any music. Those gathered there come in expectation of being changed.

Preaching is not a dead art form. Its special contribution to the mission of a church is needed as much as ever before. But some preaching is more effective than others. Today in America, one is likely to find the most effective preaching happening among churches that have stayed close to the apostolic style of ministry. These can be described as Evangelical. These preachers can teach how to stay in better contact with the audience by continually striving to gain and hold their attention with life-changing impact.

THE DANGER OF SACRAMENTALISM

Lutheran understanding of the Christ's Real Presence in communion is a matter of unchangeable substance. The frequency of celebration, however, is changeable style. The frequency has indeed changed in Lutheran churches of recent generations. For centuries the norm was celebration four times a year. Then many congregations shifted to monthly, which is still the practice among 15% of Lutheran congregations. Within living memory the norm then shifted to semi-monthly, which is the current practice of 45%, and then weekly, which describes 40% of all Lutheran congregations today.

At the same time, the norm for length of sermon went from over half an hour to less than fifteen minutes, while pastors who view the preached Word as most important in a worship service decreased from near unanimity to only three out of ten.

One can make the case that never before in the history of Lutheranism, including Luther's generation at Wittenberg, has the time devoted to preaching regularly been less than the time devoted to communion in weekly worship.

Luther's generation of pastors did continue the practice of the weekly mass, and they urged all in attendance to partake. But according to liturgical scholar John White, the lay people in reality continued their practice of participating only several times a year.[8] Most other times they were observers of what remained a very quick distribution, so that considerably less time was devoted to celebration of the sacrament than to the sermon.

And the mass form did not stay dominant. Within several decades after the Reformation a preaching service supplanted the mass in many jurisdictions. German scholar Paul Graff provides a detailed overview of

82

the history of Lutheran worship forms, and he documents from church orders over the centuries what from his viewpoint amounts to the "deterioration" of worship forms.[9] Undoubtedly the pastors and people making those simplifications saw their work as progress, inevitably in the direction of greater emphasis on preaching. Luther scholar Franz Lau observes the variety of services in those early generations and concludes: "(The view) that the services under the influence of Luther and Wittenberg were in a majority of instances sacramental services is a historical fable and nothing more."[10]

Declining time and declining importance given to the preached Word. Weekly participation in the Lord's Supper. Accomplishing everything within one hour. If stalwart Lutheran leaders from previous centuries were to look at this situation of Lutheranism in America today, one word would come quickly to their minds—a word now seldom heard: sacramentalism. They were primed to spot Roman Catholic incursions and the sacramental excesses that went with that approach to church and ministry. Reforming the sacraments was basic to the Reformation.

Sacramentalism In The
Lord's Supper

According to the *Lutheran Cyclopedia*, sacramentalism is "a designation applied to the tendency found in the Roman Catholic Church and in other bodies with a strong hierarchical trend to give to the Sacraments, specifically the Eucharist, a relatively higher inherent saving power than the Word. The tendency usually accompanies externalism in some form or other."[11]

The issue is relative importance of the preached Word and the celebrated Supper. At stake is what kind of relationship to God individual Christians are led to develop. Is it a personal relationship based on exercise of knowledge, will and conscious faith? Then basic is providing fresh perspectives on God's promises, his ways, and his expectations of those who follow him. This is the function of the sermon, the preached Word offering comfort and challenge to the lives of those present.

Or is it mostly a symbolic relationship that is dispensed as a quantity which can formally and objectively change the recipient regardless of what the person makes out of this experience with the sacred? Then the preached Word can be secondary, or at least of no greater importance.

There is danger in the direction of increased reliance on the sacraments to carry the pastoral weight of stimulating and supporting a congregation of Christians growing in their faith. The Lutheran Confessions call it doing the sacraments *ex opere operato*, by a work having been worked, as if there is operative power by the simple performance of the sacramental act. The term shows up on page after page of the Confessions, with staunch denial that the sacraments could have value *ex opere operato*. A better translation today would be "magic," the belief that by simply saying a formula of words something supernatural will happen. Indeed the magic incantation "hocus pocus" has its roots in the Latin words medieval jugglers heard but did not understand at the consecration of the elements in the Roman Catholic mass.

To point out danger in the direction of increased reliance on the sacraments is not the same as charging broad scale sacramentalism in Lutheran churches today. The Reformation heritage is still too strong for that. But what about individual pastors who rely heavily on the eucharist at the expense of the proclaimed Word? And what about the participants? What is the traditional Lutheran lay person thinking whose only contact with the Word is hearing a weak ten-minute homily in preparation for the big event? Are there many Lutheran lay people who think something magical is happening when they go forward for the bread/body and wine/blood? Almost certainly.

The Lutheran corrective to magical sacramental thinking has always been reliance on perspective provided by the strongly preached Word. The shift toward the centuries-long practice of having communion only once every three months was regarded as progress because it not only provided more opportunity for the preached Word but also gave more pastoral opportunity to assure individual preparation. At its best, the quarterly celebration was accompanied by visitation of the pastor with every communicant for a time of preparation to receive the sacrament worthily.

Dangerous Excesses

As discussed in chapter 4, Lutheran church leaders today find themselves looking in either of two directions for ideas on church life. One is toward catholic tradition, which has been very influential among Lutherans in recent decades. The other is toward Evangelicals, who have had much more influence on general American spiritual life today and specifically on Lutheran church leaders committed to church growth.

There is danger in either direction.

The danger toward Evangelical emphases are extremes of subjective emotionalism and the loss of certainty of salvation. Saving faith can be made dependent on feelings of faith, which can be high one week and low the next, leaving the individual uncertain about whether he or she truly qualifies. Such teaching is present among strains of Evangelicals that follow Arminian theology, exemplified by John Wesley's Methodism and various Pentecostal offshoots. The danger is real. The corrective is powerful preaching on the objective certainty of the Gospel promise and faithful application of the sacraments, with their conveyance of the objective certainty of God's saving action toward us.

The danger toward catholic tradition is extremes of objective magical thinking that leave the personal subjective faith of the participant undeveloped and unchallenged. The Reformers saw this danger in the Roman Catholicism of their times, and the dangerous excess is still present in Roman Catholicism today. The corrective for the Reformers was to elevate the importance of powerful preaching on personal faith as the basis of relationship with God. That is still the corrective today.

Weekly celebration with ten-minute homilies ought to be setting off warning bells and ought to shift the burden of proof to the celebrants that they are not fostering faith-crippling magical understandings. It is appropriate to ask how they are averting sacramentalism.

Warning bells are also appropriate for those of us who appreciate some aspects of Evangelical style. We should carry the burden of proof that we are not fostering subjective emotionalism. The place to look for that proof is in sermons and in teaching and use of the sacraments.

Catholic-oriented traditionalists insist on claiming that you cannot change Lutheran style without changing Lutheran substance. The position here is that much more can be changed than they think. But in respect to frequency of communion they may be right. Change the style from quarterly to weekly celebration accompanied by short sermons, and for many participants the substance of their end of the relationship with God may shift from a deepening personal faith toward a faith that stays mostly symbolic.

Sacramentalism In Baptism

The danger of sacramentalism exists with style changes in presenting the Lutheran substance of baptism, too. The major Christian radio station in Cleveland, part of the Moody network, several years ago dropped the Lutheran Hour from its broadcast schedule. The reason was listener complaints about the frequent reference to baptism as a basis for faith.

A worthwhile study for somebody would be to compare a sampling of Lutheran Hour sermons today with a sampling of those preached by Walter A. Maier fifty years ago. Undoubtedly the reference to baptism has increased. The style has changed.

What the radio audience hears is sacramentalism—attributing more saving power to the sacrament than to the Word. When Lutherans say baptism, we have the catechism definition in mind: It is not the water that does such great things, but the word of God which is in and with the water, and faith, which trusts such word of God in the water. What Evangelicals have in mind is a Roman Catholic ritual done with babies that circumvents the spiritual need for personal faith in the promises of God's Word.

Evangelicals still heed the Reformation caution against magical, *ex opere operato* sacramentalism. Are Luther's descendants today still resistant to such excesses? At a minimum, many Lutheran preachers have difficulty communicating what they mean, or what the Confessions say they should mean. The Apostle Peter's statement "Baptism now saves you" is capable of several interpretations. The best is that it is part of the mystery of how God lays claim on his spiritual followers. Never for Lutherans has it meant a water ritual that by itself guarantees heaven for a life time, as if "once baptized, always saved." Yet increasingly Lutheran abbreviated language seems to suggest such an interpretation, or at least seems to leave such an interpretation possible.

We know that in times of doubt Martin Luther used to remind himself, "I was baptized." He meant the phrase as reliance on the promise of justification by grace through faith. His relationship with God did not depend on Martin's actions toward God; God first reached out toward him at his infant baptism. God initiated this relationship, not Martin. What a comfort to someone who feels the need to appease God. The phrase "I was baptized" is rich with meaning — for someone with a mature faith like Luther's.

The focus of this chapter is on better communication. What gets communicated when a pastor offers a family the assurance that their loved one "was baptized"? I had occasion to think about this in a real-life situation. While my sister and I were in the hospital waiting room during our mother's surgery, a mother and adult daughter sat down next to me. Soon their pastor arrived, and it became apparent that their husband and father was near death from an accident. The pastor was compassionate and reassuring in talking and praying with them. Sitting one chair away, I could not help but listen. What I heard was "he was baptized" as the most fundamental reassurance of his eternal welfare. Later I learned the pastor was a well-respected Lutheran.

That the man was baptized is certainly consolation, especially as a starting point. But if the man near death had given adult evidence of saving faith, even minimally through involvement in worship and church life, then recent testimony would seem more reassuring to the family than what was done to him as an infant. If there was no adult evidence to go on, then comfort in infant baptism is something to hang onto. But reliance for an adult's salvation on an act done forty or fifty years earlier borders on sacramentalism.

TOWARD BETTER
COMMUNICATION IN WORSHIP

The sacraments are wonderful ways God has designed to communicate his saving Word to his people. In recent generations Lutherans have learned how to use them in new and improved ways in church life.

But baptism and the Lord's supper are only some of the ways God makes contact with his people as they come together in worship. The sacraments are expressions of his Word, which remains primary. God means for his Word to be communicated well, to have an impact on those who hear and experience it. The characteristics of those receiving this Word determine to a great extent how it should be communicated to be effective. A style of worship for mature Christians will likely be different from that which is effective with new Christians or those who are newly interested.

Because of such differences among those gathered, there is no one style of worship that is best for all. The apostles adapted their approach to the communication needs of those they were reaching. So should followers of apostolic style today. For new and immature Christians the well preached Word is basic.

---

1 David S. Luecke, *The Other Story of Lutherans at Worship, Fellowship Ministries*, 1995.
2 Luecke, p. 45.
3 Gracia Grindal, *"On the Decline of Preaching," Worship Innovations*, Spring 1996, p. 12.
4 David S. Luecke, *"Trends Among Lutheran Preachers," Word and World,* Volume XIX, Number 1, Winter 1999, Luther Seminary, St. Paul, Minnesota, pp 21-29.
5 Gracia Grindal, op. cit., p. 12.
6 Eugene A. Nida, *Message and Mission: The Communication of the Christian Faith,* Harper and Row, 1960, p. 74.
7 Ibid.

8 James F. White, *Protestant Worship: Traditions in Transition,* Westminster/John Knox Press, 1989, p. 42.

9 Paul Graff, Geschichte der Aufloesung der alten gottesdienstlichen Formen in der evangelischen Kirche Deutschlands, Gottingen, Vandenhoeck and Ruprecht, 1939.

10 Franz Lau, Luther, Westminister, 1963, p. 100.

11 Lutheran Cyclopedia, Concordia Publishing House, 1954, p. 935.

CHAPTER 10

Better Communication Through Personal Faith Expressions

"Frank, would you please close the meeting with prayer," the council president asked. In most traditional Lutheran churches the council president would rarely make such a request when Frank is lay person. Frank is likely to be quite uncomfortable expressing a spontaneous prayer in his own words. Almost always the request is made to the pastor. When the pastor is not present, how many committee meetings end with no prayer at all?

The larger topic of this chapter is better communication—with God and with others—through personal faith expressions. A weakness of traditional Lutheran style is the reluctance of the typical Lutheran church member to express her or her own faith in personal terms to someone else. Sharing the faith is something characteristically left to the church professionals to do. This discomfort limits the total amount of communication of the faith that Christians raised with Lutheran style do between and beyond themselves.

Where Evangelical Christians often do God talk when they are together, Lutherans too typically do only social small talk. In this respect traditional Lutheran church members are like Roman Catholics, and it is hard to see a strength in such reticence to talk about personal faith in God.

This condition calls for effort in Lutheran churches to develop a better communication style through more personal faith expressions by all participants. Beneficial outcomes would be more evangelistic witnessing, more shared personal prayer, and greater personal confidence in faith.

The precedent for apostolic, early-church communication style was set soon after Pentecost when Peter and John were speaking to the people in ways that greatly disturbed the Jewish leaders. These two were not church professionals at this point, for they were seen as "unschooled, ordinary men." They could not be forced into silence, "for we cannot help speaking about what we have seen and heard" (Acts 4:20). Later when Peter escaped from prison, he went to a house "where many people had gathered and were praying" (Acts 12:12).

In how many traditional Lutheran churches today are there gatherings of people just to pray over a special need? Prayer meetings are simply not traditional Lutheran style. Isn't that a weakness to be overcome?

How many traditional Lutheran lay people are there who could stand up and give an account of what they have seen and heard in relation to Christ's meaning for their lives? Inability and unwillingness to do so are not their fault. Such reluctance is an understandable outcome of the communication style of the Lutheran churches in which they were raised. Seldom are they called on to do God-talk. Rather the emphasis is on talking about God the right way, which is best left to the professional. Why risk saying something wrong?

One new development in LCMS circles is shaping a style of communication that actually makes this problem worse. It is a perspective that has to be resisted and overcome to make progress toward better communication through personal faith expressions.

Lex orandi, lex credendi is a Latin phrase I had never heard until receiving criticism of the book ten years ago. Then it was used like a club to denounce a violation of the "well known" theological principle *lex orandi, lex credendi*. This apparently is a teaching of late in Lutheran seminaries.

Attributed to various medieval theologians, my source traces the principle back to Pope Celestine I in the fifth century. Literally the phrase means "the rule of prayer is the rule of faith." The idea becomes more apparent when translated as "what you pray is what you believe." In current application the phrase is supposed to mean that you better watch out how you pray because imprecise prayers could mess up your faith.

Orandi, the activity of prayer, is extended to include worship. Therefore all the words in worship have to be carefully controlled. There is no room for informality, spontaneity, or departures from the liturgy. If you pray and worship in Evangelical style, you may soon lose your true Lutheran faith. So goes the argument I heard repeatedly.

Having had years to think about it, I offer three reasons why this newly announced, club-like principle is bad and has to be resisted. It isn't Lutheran. It impoverishes prayer and witnessing. It cripples faith.

Striking to me was how *lex orandi, lex credendi* was presented as a well known theological principle that needed no justification. I have yet to hear a base for it in the Lutheran Confessions—a silence especially significant from people who call themselves Confessional Lutherans and cite them at the drop of a hat. Nor have I heard a scriptural reference, which explains why it is not in the Confessions.

Have the rules for defining Lutheran changed in this past generation? I suspect this has happened to seminary teaching in the absence of serious challenge from the church at large. How else would a prudent caution turn into a style-defining mandate. Isn't it worrisome that the authority for the alleged mandate is a Catholic pope?

IMPOVERISHED PRAYER AND WITNESSING

The reason this principle could go unchallenged is that it describes what Lutheran style practices turned into over the centuries. But this is for sociological reasons, not theological. Luther himself had great confidence that lay people could read the Bible and express its truths on their own. He even offered "the mutual conversation and consolation of the brethren" as a fifth means of grace (Smalcald Articles, Part 3, Article 4).

In state-run village churches, growing up Lutheran meant memorizing the Catechism and sitting through worship services that followed the same "agenda" of formal expressions week after week. These were offered as the right way to talk about God. The implication is that other ways are wrong. To depart from the formal expressions was to risk reprimand from the pastor, whose identity as teacher was important to all. For the pastor to depart from the formalities of the agenda was to risk reprimand from the state-church consistory, which was expected by the prince or ruler to keep "his" church under careful control.

German Lutheranism was shaped in a German culture that was (and still is) unusually control oriented. The practical lesson learned in church life was: Don't say anything you don't have to, lest you get faulted for saying it wrong. Too often another lesson learned was: Don't do anything more than you have to, lest you do it wrong or for the wrong reason. I believe this impoverishment was an unintended consequence of culture, not theology.

That Lutherans do not pray out loud in public is evident even among pastors gathered informally for a meal in a restaurant. Most will pause to offer a silent personal prayer and occasionally several will join with subdued voice in the "Come, Lord Jesus" table prayer. But few feel comfortable voicing a spontaneous prayer loud enough to be heard a table away. Isn't this part of a Lutheran style that represents a weakness and not a strength?

In the chapter on "More Personal Faith Expressions" ten years ago, I was focused on the mission impact of increased personal expressions of faith. For someone not used to expressing God-talk, witnessing the faith to a stranger is intimidating. My suggestion was that an easier place to start is talking with God through shared prayer. Since that time I have done many half-day prayer encounters that have helped traditional Lutherans overcome their inhibitions toward public prayer. Most never had such an experience before. Isn't it odd that prayer retreats or even prayer meetings are almost completely missing from our inherited Lutheran church style today? Shouldn't that be changed?

THE LANGUAGE OF EXPERIENCE

One reason traditional Lutherans are reluctant to give witness to their faith is that the communication modeled for us is mostly doctrinal preachments supported with Bible passages. Carefully formulated doctrine is a great strength of Lutheranism. But this specialized language is more suited to professionals and often leaves lay people uncertain about whether they are "saying it right." This propositional language too often becomes preachy and boring.

An alternative used by many other Christians over the centuries is experiential language—expressing faith in terms of personal experience. Such language has phrases like: This is what God did in my life. Here is how I found new peace in the Lord. I found new meaning in the Gospel when....

This was the language of Peter and John when they could not help speaking about what they had seen and heard. It was the language of the apostolic church of first-generation Christians who told about their conversion and explained why their new faith was so compelling to them. Compared to doctrinal language, experiential language is usually expressed with more intensity and conviction. Personal faith stories are more effective at stimulating others to explore the faith further. That is what front-line witnessing is all about. The doctrinal language of propositions remains necessary to the understanding God's ways. The ideal is to become bilingual, to present objective truth illustrated with subjective experience.

Experiential language is easier for the non-specialist to talk. But it assumes someone has a religious experience to share. The most-told kind of experience is how someone was "born again" and became a Christian. The Apostle Paul told his born-again story in Acts 22. Evangelicals today receive constant encouragement to tell their stories, which can be very interesting and faith building. However, few Lutherans can talk about their conversion. Most were born into the church. We were born again of the Holy Spirit at our baptism as infants.

But infant baptism does not mean that Lutherans have little religious experience to share. They just receive little encouragement to recognize and describe God's actions in their personal lives over the years. Instead of conversion, Lutherans can talk about personal awakenings. This style of communicating has ample precedent in Lutheran heritage, albeit a style that is lost from memory.

When getting to know individual Lutherans better, I have found it productive to inquire about when they felt closest to God, or what they remember as a mountain-top spiritual experience, or when their faith meant the most to them. There is usually initial hesitance. But then most can talk about a special time when they moved to a new understanding of God perhaps in their grief at the death of someone close, or how their faith took on more depth when they were incapacitated or had lost a job, or how they discovered a new relationship with God when something knocked them out of control of their life. There really are a lot of interesting "awakening" stories out there among traditional Lutherans.

The best example in Scripture of this kind of spiritual awakening is the story of the two followers of Jesus walking home to Emmaus on Easter. Described as disciples of Christ, they reviewed the events of the weekend with a walking companion we know to be Jesus. But they did not recognize him. Then as the stranger broke bread with them came the moment they must have talked about the rest of their lives. "Then their eyes were opened and they recognized him" (Luke 24:31). Everything was the same as it had been for hours. It was their perception that had been changed. An awakening had happened to them. Imagine the witness they gave over the years.

The Apostle Paul in Romans 12:2 talks about continuing to be transformed by the renewing of our minds. There can be many transformations and renewals in the Christian's long life with Christ. Each is worth talking about.

He taught the Corinthians that "We, who with unveiled faces all reflect the Lord's glory, are being transformed into his likeness with ever increasing glory, which comes from the Lord, who is the Spirit" (2 Corinthians 3:18). The person who in faith has turned to Christ has the veil removed that prevents him or her from reflecting any of God's glory. Having the veil removed is the one-time act of being justified before God. Then comes a repeated process of being changed, or experiencing transformation—being awakened—that restores more of the glorious image of God in the believer's new life here on earth.

The hope, inheritance, and power available in Christ are right there in front of all believers. But many spend most of their lives recognizing only a part of how much difference this hope and power can make in their lives right now. For some there is a gradual growth. But for others there are growth spurts that they can associate with a special experience, or a new relationship, or a personal crisis. The Holy Spirit works in many ways.

Given an opportunity, many Christians, including traditional Lutherans, can tell about awakenings that are well worth sharing.

Telling awakening stories used to be a very Lutheran thing to do. "Tell me about your first awakening" was a question routinely asked by Henry Melchior Muhlenberg, the major leader of Lutheranism in America in the eighteenth century.[1] The Lutheran Church—Missouri Synod was born out of an Awakening movement in Germany in the early nineteenth century. The Synod's second president, Friedrich Wyneken, talked frequently about coming from an "awakened" family and talked about "awakened" associates.[2]

So long as personal experiences are shared in a context that appreciates and shares doctrinal truths, there should be no change in Lutheran substance. But what an improvement in style of communication.

Wouldn't it be neat if Lutherans started telling awakening stories again?

STUNTED FAITH

Learning the language of personal experience can also deepen personal faith.

A new language is easiest learned when a child. But the language of religious experience usually becomes possible only after childhood. While doctrine can be memorized, often with little understanding, personal stories have to be individually thought up and told in order to take on their meaning and shape. The language of personal faith has to be used to be learned.

I learned German after childhood. I thought I knew a fair amount after two years of high school and four years of college German. But when I decided to study in Germany after college, I had to face the fact that I could not converse in the language. This realization led me to a West Coast German summer school where the language was spoken and then to a semester at the translator's school of the University of Heidelberg where I studied. Then I was able to do at least basic communication in writing and speech. Since then I have found that fluency in a different language continues only through regularly using it.

I think this principle applies to the language of faith, too. It is true that saving faith does not have to be articulated to be in effect; such faith is simple trust of God's Gospel promises. But for that faith to expand into the foundation for changing daily life and giving powerful witness to others, it needs to be regularly used in communication. The believer needs to express his or her faith in words that have personal meaning.

94

What are the consequences when Christians receive little encouragement to articulate their faith in words that come naturally and easily? They
may wind up with a daily faith that has little impact on the way they live
their lives. Unexpressed faith is likely to be stunted faith.

With regard to Lutheran Christians, consider the findings from peri-
odic surveys. The most recent is Lutheran Brotherhood's 1998 "Survey of
Lutheran Beliefs and Practices."

Only 57% agreed with the pivotal Lutheran teaching that "Only those
who believe in Jesus Christ as their savior can go to heaven." But half of
those who agreed with this statement also agreed that "God is satisfied if a
person lives the best life one can"—a teaching that has to be wrong if the
previous one is right. Only one out of four found fault with the statement
that "The main emphasis of the Gospel is on God's rules for right living"—
another statement that has to be wrong if the first one is right.

Rare would be Lutheran pastors who say they are preaching anything
other than justification by grace through faith. Yet little more than only half
the hearers recognize how salvation happens. Less than one out of three
understands the implications for daily living.

Whatever else is going on, there is clearly a communication gap between what Lutheran pastors and teachers intend to communicate and what
actually comes across to those who are sitting through sermons and lessons. Much of this outcome can be attributed to a style of teaching and
therefore a style of learning.

Through centuries Lutherans have preached and taught to mostly cap-
tive audiences. To be a respected village dweller meant you went to the
village church and sent your children to the village catechism classes. The
social pressure to do so was high.

The pastors and teachers were paid from endowments and state funds
and were not dependent on members for much of their livelihood. They
did their job by passing on the faith at the assigned times in the careful
language of the true doctrine they were held accountable to by supervisors
who determined their destiny. The people did their job by showing up for
church on Sundays and listening to religious language that was typically
quite different from their language of daily life. Having small group discussions to probe deeper meanings was in many cases forbidden, for fear
of fostering churches within the church.

How much actually got communicated was not important to this ritual
pattern. Church and community life went on from generation to generation
regardless. Only in this country did Lutherans become forced to assess the

worth of what they receive in terms of dollars they are willing to contribute financially for the experience.

Village dynamics of ritual church life carried on well into the twentieth century in the churches of Lutherans in America. That came with being an ethnic church, be it German, Norwegian, or whatever nationality. Those churches are now for the most part seeing the third generation of members to grow up without the mother tongue and without the identity such ethnicity gave. Loyalties have receded, and the church ritual by itself is not nearly so compelling anymore.

Teaching Style

The changing social context of the twenty-first century calls for a change in characteristic teaching style among Lutheran pastors. Commissioned Lutheran teachers with training in the field of education have for the most part made that change. Lutheran pastors, though, have been unusually oriented to the lecture style where all that was important was told to people who just listened. This approach can be very time saving and easily controlled. However, in their inherited church culture outside their schools, Lutherans developed few techniques for consistent feedback and assessment of what was actually being learned by those who sat passively before the pastor.

Lecture style teaching has its strengths and place. Well done, one-way lectures can stimulate interest among hearers and convey important knowledge. But the impact of this style is confined mostly to head knowledge. For really serious teaching, lecture is usually combined with some form of feedback of understanding, like discussion and testing.

What lectures cannot do well by themselves is to change attitudes and perspectives. This is an assumption basic to the kind of teaching I did for years in programs that intended to shape the perceptions and skills of those who wanted to manage working relationships with others. For that purpose the learner needs to compare his or her understanding to the reactions and insights of others. Discussion of cases and incidents becomes a basic teaching tool. In this setting the students have not learned something until they are able to express and put it to use on their own.

While traditional Lutheran culture did not develop feedback techniques for what was being learned through preaching and teaching, modern survey studies can now provide that function. As reported earlier, the news is not good. The majority of Lutherans are fuzzy on the implications of

God's relationship with them based on his grace rather than on their own accomplishments.

Would many recognize the impact of the Gospel better if they found themselves more often in situations where they tried to express it in words that come naturally? Undoubtedly. There are many ways to do that. My experience is that the easiest and least threatening approach is to encourage Lutherans to talk directly to God out loud with others. Praying their faith amounts to trying it out, and when they do so in the presence of others, they can receive encouragement and counsel. This is the strength Luther recognized in the "mutual conversation and consolation of brethren" that he highly recommended—as a means of grace no less.

TOWARD BETTER COMMUNICATION THROUGH PERSONAL FAITH EXPRESSIONS

Lex orandi, lex credendi (What you pray is what you believe) has no standing as a Lutheran doctrine. But it does offer wisdom worth thinking about. The phrase can also be reversed: *lex credendi, lex orandi.* If you believe it you will pray it. Could it be that if you do not pray something by expressing it yourself, you probably do not believe it?

Think of the vitality that could happen in Lutheran churches that would concentrate on improving communication through personal faith expressions in prayer and witness—done by the many, not just the hired few.

While Lutherans typically do not express spontaneous prayer thoughts out loud in front of others, most do carry on significant personal prayer lives. This is something I was happy to discover in a 1993 survey of prayer practices among Missouri Synod Lutherans in 105 different congregations across the country. One question I had was how many of the 548 respondents prayed daily. Because I saw in public so little evidence of personal prayer, my initial guess was perhaps one out of four did daily prayer other than at meals. Most pastors I shared this study with made an initial guess in this low range. The result turned out to be a much higher three out of four. Almost all respondents said they prayed in their own words.[3]

What a strong base for building prayer ministry in a congregation! Think of the encouragement of one another and the strengthened fellowship that could grow when many join in bringing shared prayer out of the their spiritual closets. Think of the increased blessings that could flow from increased petitions. Is the routine confinement of prayer to personal privacy a necessary part of Lutheran substance? Rather, isn't supplementing private prayer with shared prayer a matter of style that can and should be improved?

97

One of the best ways to help Lutherans overcome their inherited reluctance to share faith expression is to help them pray out loud to God in the presence of others. Shared prayer can open the way for sharing personal faith experiences.

---

1 "The Documentary History of the Evangelical Lutheran Ministerium of Pennsylvania and Adjacent States, 1748-1821," *Christian History*, Vol. V, No. 2, p. 32.
2 Norman J. Threinen, "F.C.D. Wyneken: Motivator for the Mission, "*Concordia Theological Quarterly*, January-April, 1996, p. 21.
3 David S. Luecke, *Talking With God: How Ordinary Christians Grow in Prayer*, Fellowship Ministries, 1997.

CHAPTER 11

Better Organizing Of Church Life

The 1950s were a time of great growth for Lutheran church bodies in America, as it was for almost all church bodies. Energy pent up during the Depression and World War II was released in wide-spread migration to the suburbs. Church planting happened on an unprecedented scale. District, synod, and national administrative units added staff, bought bigger buildings, and turned part-time presidencies into full-time positions.

Bigger was indeed better then in just about any organized activity, be it industrial corporations, school districts, governments, or television networks. Resources were plentiful, and the advantage went to efforts that gained efficiencies through merging resources into bigger organizations. Lutheran charities of all sorts came together for a united appeal throughout metropolitan areas. What constituted better organization was easy to recognize and support.

The path to better organization of church life going into the twenty-first century is harder to recognize and even harder to make persuasive. In a way, smaller is now better. Huge business corporations have been a source of loss of jobs through downsizing. The fast pace of growth of the economy is being driven by small enterprises. Where top graduates of business schools in the 1960s opted for careers in large corporations, they now set off to start their own business. This is the age of the entrepreneur.

So it is in church life, too. The growth is with entrepreneurial congregations and their pastor leaders. In the 1950s growth happened through district-financed multiplication of small congregations. Now, what little growth there is happens mostly with the small proportion of large congregations that are getting larger—a trend reflected in the doubling of the number of congregations that bring in 35 or more adult confirmands a year, as reported in chapter 2. Where pastors used to look to district and synod for program ideas, they now gather to learn from trend-setting congregations like Community Church of Joy in Phoenix or Willow Creek Community Church in the Chicago area. The consistent message of these teaching churches is that each congregation has to find its own way with what works best to accomplish its purpose in its own community.

Implicit in this shift from national to local is acceptance of greater diversity. A point of pride in the 1950s was that you could go into any congregation in a church body like the LCMS and they would be worshiping in the same format with the same texts as any other congregations. You could be spiritually at home wherever you were. Now congregations, especially the growing ones, have many styles of worship. It is the trend toward diversification that Lutherans in particular are having a hard time accepting.

Momentum toward centralization brings greater control. Momentum toward decentralization means loss of control. Loosely controlled, grassroots efforts seem messy, and Lutherans have a strong instinct toward well-controlled good order.

GREATER DIVERSITY TO
ACCOMMODATE INCREASED OPTIONS

Thus it is important to understand the underlying reasons for the trend toward better organization through decentralization and diversity, in churches as well as in other organizations. The current direction is not just a passing fad.

Veteran church observer Lyle Schaller offers a simple illustration of what is happening. He describes a woman who used to come early to church meetings to make coffee. But she finally gave up what had become too complicated. Twenty years ago all that was involved was coming early and getting a pot of coffee started. "Now," she says, "some want decaffeinated, others want regular coffee, a few insist on tea, some want a soft drink, others ask for fruit juice, and there always will be some who wants hot chocolate. I say let them make their own or go without."[1]

Churches, of course, could say, "We offer only regular coffee; take it or leave it." Or they could say, "We offer no refreshments." But subtle, positive things happen when members see a recognition and affirmation of their preferences. An interesting study would be to compare attendance at meetings with diverse refreshments to attendance when just coffee is served and then to attendance where no refreshments at all are served. The actual form of refreshment would probably not be as important as the attitude conveyed by providing choices.

We live in a culture that multiplies choices at an increasing rate. More alternatives for refreshment are easy to recognize. So is the increasing number of offerings on cable television, with the result that the major broadcast networks are fighting a losing battle to maintain their viewership. Retail stores get bigger to accommodate offering a greater variety of products. College-bound students expect a choice of many different majors, and colleges struggle to expand offerings without diminishing quality. Where once a telephone and the U.S. Mail were sufficient for communication, we now expect those we call to have an answering machine, plus a fax and e-mail. Someone who goes without any of these is increasingly at a disadvantage.

Grocery stores are a good place to check out the loss of brand loyalty that goes with increased choice. Whatever the product, there are always other brands that promise better quality, more convenience, or lower prices coupled with inducements to try something else. So it is with automobiles.

So it is also with churches in metropolitan areas. Old brand loyalties are disappearing. For people looking for a church, denominational brand loyalty is being replaced by new practical considerations of how well individual preferences are met. Making this statement does not mean that church life *should* be this way. It just recognizes the new realities mission-minded churches have to deal with.

My study of preaching and worship trends in Lutheran churches brought to light a relationship that supports the importance of diversity in worship. Of the congregations that offered two or more services on a weekend, those that use different service formats are more than twice as likely to report growth in attendance than those that do the same in all services. This observation says nothing about what the choices might be. Just the availability of an alternative made a difference. In itself the attitude reflected in willingness to offer different worship formats is undoubtedly a major factor in the outcome.

UNITY IN DIVERSITY

The basic challenge of any organizing effort is to recognize important differences among component parts and then to figure out how to integrate what the parts contribute. That is straight organization theory. With too little differentiation among people and parts, the organization cannot adapt well to its environment and loses its effectiveness. With too much differentiation, the organization loses efficiency and may even splinter. Wisdom about what needs to be accomplished is the key to achieving good structural relationships, based on recognition of changes to which the organization has to adapt.

Church bodies are not exempt from the need to rearrange relationships between their parts. Seldom in any human effort is one organizational arrangement best in all circumstances and times. Especially in a period of fast social change like that occurring in America today, all organizations have to review, change, and fine tune their structural relationships repeatedly. This is true for congregations and church bodies, too. Increased differentiation is the response called for today.

The Biblical expression for this effort is to strive to maintain unity in the midst of diversity. The unity of God's people is a basic theme of Scripture. But the New Testament approach to unity placed the emphasis differently than did the Old Testament. The children of Israel sought to express their unity through binding rules and laws spelled out in great detail. The goal was to demonstrate their distinctive identity and unity as God's special people by a basic uniformity of dress, meals, ritual, and, through circumcision, even bodily markings. That was God's old covenant of Law— the one that he changed when he turned his people into the new, Gospel-based body of Christ.

Insisting on uniformity is an easily understood, simple approach to achieve unity. I remember a debate from church-college days about whether congregations should be encouraged to sing hymns in four-part harmony. To some, that reflected a loss of unity. They preferred to insist on the uniformity of all singing the melody. In the process they missed out on the wonderful blessings of harmony. Church leaders with such high regard for uniformity must be having a miserable time with the current trend toward diversity in worship.

Uniformity is highly valued in the German culture from which most Lutherans came. As one extreme example, I remember seeing a movie in German on the life of Friedrich Schiller in the eighteenth century. Included in showing his military training was a scene of all the soldiers being in their bunks ready to sleep at the same time, with all lying on their right side with their left arm out from under the cover. That's uniformity!

In God's new covenant presented in the New Testament, the understanding of unity is much more subtle. Diversity is celebrated. That is the main point of Paul's challenging teaching in 1 Corinthians 12. In Christ's church there are different kinds of gifts, different kinds of service, different abilities to perform service, but the same Spirit, the same Lord, the same God works all of them in all men. The body is considerably strengthened by such God-given diversity. Paul was apparently quite willing to rely on the Spirit who gave this diversity to also bring unity out of it. He confesses,

"We were all baptized by one Spirit into one body, and we were all given the one Spirit to drink." Unity is maintained by something greater than Law-based resolutions and rules enforced through raw political process. He told the Ephesians to make every effort to keep the unity of the Spirit through the bond of peace.

Can the principle of different contributions from different people be extended to different ministry emphases by different congregations, based on the gifts given them by the Spirit and on their community circumstances? Instead of grudgingly conceding diversity, a Pauline church body would enthusiastically promote and celebrate it.

In recent decades many Lutheran pastors have been discovering the practical value of Paul's teaching on spiritual gifts in 1 Corinthians 12, Romans 12, and Ephesians 4. This Biblical recognition of the diversity of Spirit-given gifts that are present among members in a congregation can become for church leaders today the conceptual foundation for engaging an increasing number of individuals in fellowship-building ministries that are personally gratifying to them as well as pleasing to God.

Such practical application of the apostolic teaching on spiritual gifts remains controversial in Lutheran circles. This application is not part of Lutheran tradition. But does that mean it is unLutheran? Clearly it is scriptural, and in congregation after congregation God does bless it. Let the tradition be stretched!

Diversity at Royal Redeemer includes five weekend worship services in four different formats. To plan and lead these services is a real challenge for the staff. We are learning to think of the attendees at each service time as a separate congregation. What brings about unity among the five congregations in one location? Besides unity in message and staff, we find that the overall mission of reaching the unchurched provides the glue that holds the larger congregation together. Without that outward thrust, the frictions that develop between traditional and contemporary participants could easily erupt into unity-destroying conflict.

Unity in the apostolic church was something the Holy Spirit achieved through bringing recognition of the common mission to spread the Gospel. The Spirit stands ready to use common mission to acheve unity today, too.

APOSTOLIC STYLE OF ORGANIZING

How did the apostolic church organize itself? As with worship, the topic of organization was apparently not important enough to write about

103

directly. There is no clear organization chart that we can replicate. What we can learn comes mostly from observation of churches in action. Little consistency is apparent beyond encouragement to solve problems and to be orderly. Leaving synagogue structure behind, the apostles approached their leadership tasks with a freedom to choose organizational forms that furthered their ministry purposes.

In the book of Acts we find elders to be key workers alongside the apostles. Yet in his letters the Apostle Paul seldom mentions elders and focuses on overseers and deacons. He mentions pastors only in a passing reference where they are associated with teachers. Tradition projects back on apostolic times an organization revolving around bishop (overseers), elders, and deacons. Over centuries the word for elder (*presbyteros*) turned into priest, and we have the classic Catholic hierarchy of bishop, priest, and deacon. All others were just "people," who by tradition are called laity, a term that comes from *laos*, which is the common Greek word for "people."

But nowhere is there a place where these three levels of leadership are presented together. The Greek word for clergy (*kleros*) is not applied to leaders. While there were important distinctions among leaders and differing expectations for them, nowhere does the New Testament present a recognition of just two classes of Christians: clergy and laity. In their freedom in choice of organizational form, groups of churches can certainly take on a hierarchical structure of clearly delineated offices and authority. In freedom, they can sharply distinguish between a leadership class (clergy) and everybody else, who are treated as followers. But churches making such choices cannot defend them as the only Biblical pattern. Church bodies remain free to select other organizational relationships that make the most sense for the ministry they are trying to accomplish.

My own conclusion is that the Biblical word for elder can best be translated as "leader" in the generic sense today of anyone who leads, without necessarily recognizing distinctions in position. Efforts to fit the Lutheran understanding of "pastor" into Biblical organizational structure are especially tenuous; Paul's single use of the word in the Ephesians 4 listing of kinds of leaders is its only New Testament appearance as something resembling a church leadership position. The passage cited for ordination of pastors (Titus 1:5) can just as well be translated "to put order into the confusion and designate leaders in every town in Crete."

These observations about apostolic approach to leadership should not be interpreted to mean that God does not specially call and equip some for special church leadership. The point is that he raises up a variety of leaders—more than can be fitted adequately into the traditional two classes of clergy and laity. The next chapter shows how in Lutheran understandings pastors of congregations do have a distinctive, God-affirmed role that gives them special status deserving special respect. That specialness was easier to recognize in the German title of *Prediger* (preacher) and the position of *Predigtamt,* which is confusingly translated into English as the office of public ministry.

The lack of a clear organization chart with job descriptions is seen by many as a mark of the "primitive" church that had not yet developed into its best form—something which later tradition provided. But rather than regarding the apostolic church as inadequate, we can better regard it as a model for our times. That early church expanded so quickly not *in spite of* poor organization but *because of* loose organization that could be fitted to specific situations. Of paramount concern to the apostles was getting new churches started. The form could fit the circumstances and personalities. We can infer that the structure received attention only when there were problems.

This attitude of diversity of form might seem alien to Lutheran expectations. But Martin Luther himself saw the larger picture for developing congregational life. Just as he resisted designating one order of worship for all churches, he was skeptical about drawing up a detailed church order or constitution for all churches that became Lutheran. According to Vilmos Vajda, "(Luther) thought that unwritten customs should first be established before being made binding by precepts and laws. The reverse he rejected, because it implied a disregard of the existing customs within the congregation, a failure to adapt to the given situation, and the danger of legalism."[2]

CENTRALIZED OR DECENTRALIZED?

So how did the apostolic church function organizationally? Was the important action in Jerusalem or on the mission front advancing from city to city? From the New Testament we can learn some helpful lessons about maintaining a productive tension between mission-oriented congregations and unity-maintaining central authority.

The basic unit of apostolic organization was, of course, the house church. The Apostle Paul mentions the households of specific hosts, like Priscilla and Aquila, at the end of his letters to the Romans, the Corinthians, and the Philippians. There were at least three households in Rome. We gain the picture of several households in most cities where Paul established Christian presence. The households came with an already recognized leader, namely the host. We do not know what the arrangement was that brought the household churches together in a city like Rome. It was apparently not important enough to explain.

The natural headquarter for the Christian movement was Jerusalem, where the pivotal events of Jesus' death and resurrection occurred and where the Christian church was born on Pentecost. When serious conflict rose in AD 48 the apostles gathered in Jerusalem to find a solution, as reported in Acts 15 and Ephesians 2. This original church continued to have recognition as the place where Jesus would return at the end of time. But we hear about it mostly as impoverished and in need of financial support from the new churches spread over many countries. Then the Jerusalem church recedes from a central role and it disappears at the time of the destruction of the city in AD 70. Decades earlier the real base of operations had shifted for awhile to the church in Antioch.

From the viewpoint of mission vitality, the demise of the Jerusalem church can be looked at as a God-send. Of necessity the scattered churches took on more responsibility and authority. From a similar viewpoint of congregational vitality, the imprisonment and execution of Paul was a God-send. His absence empowered many others to take stronger leadership roles. A general lesson from the early church is that central authority did not figure prominently in God's plan for his New Testament people.

ATTITUDE TOWARDS TRADITION

The Apostolic Convention is pivotal for the understanding of congregations joined together in a larger unity. In the book ten years ago I described how the apostles very carefully distinguished between substance and style in order to set boundaries for churches to consider themselves part of the Christian movement. They had to decide what to do with the Jewish traditions that naturally carried over into the first church made up followers who were Jewish. Paul's mission thrust among Gentiles added believers to the movement who did not share those traditions. Could someone be a Christian without observing the Jewish traditions? The answer then was by no means apparent, and the traditionalists (Judaizers) were harassing the mission churches of Gentiles. The apostles carefully drew a line between which traditions were important and which ones could be changed (Acts 15:24-29).

A major lesson of the convention is the attitude toward traditions that drove their considerations. Peter argued for not "putting on the necks of the disciples a yoke that neither we nor our fathers have been able to bear." Chairman James announced the judgment "that we should not make it difficult for the Gentiles who are turning to God." Traditions that were not crucial to the Gospel were clearly secondary.

Much of the tension among Lutherans today is over the role of traditions, especially in worship. Some insist on maintaining traditions that go through Luther all way back to the fourth century. To them being "Lutheran" is foremost. Are their similarities between Lutheranizers and Judaizers? Others view classic traditional worship as a heavy burden to put on people coming to Christ without growing up in the tradition. Being in mission to help people become Gospel-believing Christians is foremost. The apostles' principle is clearly relevant today: Mission takes precedence over unnecessary traditions.

DECISION MAKING FOR UNITY

Another key lesson from the first convention concerns the process of organizational decision making. There was no imposition of authority by one group over the objections of the other. All kept talking until they came to agreement. True church unity is God given (1 Corinthians 12: 4-6). It must have been thrilling to the leaders at the first Christian church convention to announce, "It seemed good to the Holy Spirit and to us not to burden you with anything beyond the following requirements." What a model for church body decision making today! How can we know when church-wide decisions are pleasing to the Holy Sprit? The apostolic answer is: When everybody involved agrees it makes sense for the right Gospel-based reasons.

If the apostles opted for the freedom of diversity, what would keep the Christian movement cohesive? What would prevent splintering into hundreds of congregations that had little relation to each other? Three courses of action toward unity can be identified.

The first is apparent in the Spirit-pleasing announcement of what could not change. Gentile as well as Jewish Christians were supposed to keep kosher and not eat food sacrificed to idols. We know that Paul considered Gospel freedom to extend to what is eaten, since he wrote to the Corinthians, "But food does not bring us near to God." Yet for the sake of the larger

107

unity he gave in and accepted as binding something that was unnecessary for the Gospel.

The second way apostolic churches maintained unity is through personal relationships. Paul, Barnabas, Timothy, Titus and many other leaders traveled extensively to visit the various scattered churches. They did not rely only on convention resolutions to force compliance. They were seen as trying to help the individual churches be God-pleasing, and on that basis their personal authority was accepted. Can church unity be maintained today when trusting personal relationships among leaders are in decline, and when many congregations tend to disregard the central body as much help in pursuing the mission they hear God calling them to do in their community.

The third way to foster unity was to ask churches to help each other. Paul worked hard to raise money from his scattered congregations to help the "poor" back in Jerusalem. Some would consider this offering a tax from headquarters on its supporting churches. But Paul consistently treated it a thank offering. Most important is having the new churches recognize the larger unity by sharing their resources. In Paul's version of that first convention, as recorded in Galatians, he reports, "All they asked was that we should continue to remember the poor, the very thing I was eager to do."

Jerusalem was not in a position to demand much of anything. In fact, it was more in the position of a beggar. We do not know whether C.F.W. Walther, the founder of the Lutheran Church—Missouri Synod, had this apostolic lesson in mind. But he certainly had learned the principle. Consider his following statement of the relationship between Synod and its member congregations:

> In its self-government the congregation is free to do anything that it can defend before God, and the Synod has no say in the matter. But the Synod has the duty to give advice when asked. Therefore the Synod can establish no rules, no ceremonies, not any kind of regulations; it cannot impose taxes, not even a penny. If our Synod would ever say, "Every congregation *must* contribute one cent every year," then the congregations should say, "Not even half a cent. You must beg; yes, we'll gladly give to a beggar, but if you try to give us orders, our friendship is over. Because— whether much or little—if we have conceded you a penny this year, you can demand a dollar next year, and even more in two years; for we would have then given you the right, the power, to tell us what to do."[3]

The term "synod" has organizational implications in itself. If Lutheran founders had spoken English in the nineteenth century they would have

108

called their church body the Missouri Convention of the Lutheran Church. Convention is what the German term "synod" means. The Lutheran Church— Missouri Synod, which could be named the Missouri Lutheran Convention, is comparable in organizational structure to the Southern Baptist Convention. Convention refers to the meeting of the whole church body, done annually in the Southern Baptist Convention and now the Missouri Lutheran Convention. This structure is exactly parallel to the apostolic convention in AD 48. The bureaucracy of elected and appointed leaders has no authority beyond what the tri-annual meeting gives it. According to Walther, resolutions of the large meeting are binding only so far as the member congregations allow them to be. Like the apostolic convention, the Missouri convention has to operate on the basis of trust and agreement.

In popular use today "Synod" has come to be used as the verb "walking together." But properly it is a noun best translated as "on the same road together." There is a subtle difference between the concept of walking together and taking the same road. The verb suggests going arm-in-arm at the same pace over the same bumps and curves. The noun suggests that the road is shared but those traveling it may well be at different places encountering different challenges of the journey. Going arm-in-arm suggests uniformity. Journeys on the same road suggest that the mission—getting to the right destination—is the basis of unity. Focus on the common mission allows for diversity in how the road is traveled.

TOWARD BETTER ORGANIZING
OF CHURCH LIFE

There is no one style of organizing that is best for all congregations and all church bodies for all times. The apostles did not depend on carefully defined organization to accomplish their mission. They depended on relationships of trust and agreement among colleagues pursuing a shared mission. They agreed that reaching out as far as possible with the Gospel was their driving concern. They adapted well to the diversity that emerged among the people they were reaching.

The main organizational challenge for churches today is to recognize and adapt to increased diversity in the personal preferences of those they are trying to reach. Changes in style will increasingly originate with local congregations pursuing the mission to which they hear God calling them then and there. To remain effective today, church bodies will need to recognize and support greater diversity among their congregations and thereby also learn to function with a greater decentralization of authority. Apostolic style of organizing was very effective for the early church. It can be for churches today, too.

---

1 Lyle Schaller, *Its a Different World: The Challenges for Today's Pastor*," Abingdon Press, 1987, p. 223.

2 Vilmos Vajta, *Luther on Worship: An Interpretation*, Muhlenberg Press, 1958, p. 182.

3 C. F. W. Walther, "Duties of an Evangelical Lutheran Synod: First Iowa District Convention, St. Paul's Church, Fort Dodge, Iowa, Beginning Aug. 20, 1879," in *Essays for the Church*, Vol. 2: 1877-1886, trans. Everett W. Meier (St. Louis: CPH, 1992), 2:31-32.

CHAPTER 12

Better Organizing Of Ministry

Who is a minister in the Lutheran Church?

Ask many pastors and they will quickly say, "All members." They will point with enthusiasm to their bulletin listing of staff and its concluding line: Ministers—Everybody.

Ask some traditionalists and they will say, "Only the ordained pastor. The word 'minister' should be saved to describe this position. This is 'the ministry'. All other members are something else."

This dispute over one word reflects differing tendencies in the view of church and ministry among Lutherans, especially among Lutherans of the Missouri Synod. This particular dispute, however, probably would not happen if we still spoke German.

The issue is what to call the congregational leader who preaches, administers the sacraments, and is responsible for the spiritual dimension of church life. In German this is the *Prediger*, the preacher. The position is the *Predigtamt*, the office of preaching. The "amt" at the end of the word is a Germanism hard to translate. Literally it means "office." But the word has the connotation of a publicly recognized position. In Missouri Synod translations, *Predigtamt* came out the Office of Public Ministry, often shortened to Public Ministry.

Much was changed in the translation. What is "public ministry," and where do you find this position in Scripture? The loss of identity as preacher has had two serious consequences. One is the decline of preaching, as discussed in chapter 9. The other is loss of distinctiveness of this leadership role in the body of Christ. On the one hand, if only the pastor is called minister, many members undervalue the worth of their own contribution of ministry, to use the term in its Biblical sense of important, Christ-like service. On the other hand, if all are counted as ministers, many pastors feel their own self worth threatened by the loss of distinctiveness of their contribution, which is different from that of all the others. They then resist new ways of thinking about how all the ministries of the congregation can be better organized—the pastor's and everyone else's.

The bottom line of the book on Evangelical style and Lutheran substance was that Lutherans can learn better, more effective styles of communicating and organizing. The point of the last four chapters of this book is that these better styles are also well founded in New Testament practice. Such is an even more persuasive reason for taking them seriously.

In the previous chapter, better organizing of church life dealt with relations between smaller groupings of Christians and larger groupings, within congregations, and between congregations and associations of congregations. Organizational emphases these days are on smaller, local units that can respond more effectively to opportunities as well as to heightened expectations that personal preferences will be met.

This chapter considers how to better organize the work, that is, the ministries within the congregation. Who are the leaders? How should they relate to each other? How should the preacher/pastor relate to them?

The book ten years ago entitled this twelfth and last chapter "More Leadership by Personal Gift." This is an awkward phrase that runs the risk of communicating little. A clearer phrase would be "More Lay Ministry." But the risk there is perpetuating a simplistic distinction between clergy and laity that is not Scriptural. But ignoring that distinction, I have learned, runs the risk of communicating a diminished view of the role and importance of the called pastor. Such a conclusion would be unfortunate at a time when the role and contribution of the preacher/leader of a congregation is more important than ever before.

TOP DOWN OR BOTTOM UP?

The choice of starting point for better organizing of the ministries of a congregation can in itself determine how the organizing will be done. To start with the called pastor is to set the stage for viewing all the other members of the congregation in the support roles of helpers and housekeepers. There is still plenty of work for members to do but the pastor does the really important things.

An example of this way of thinking can be found in a Bible study that accompanies the collected essays in *Church and Ministry,* issued in 1998 by the Office of the President of the Lutheran Church—Missouri Synod. In a section on "The Royal Priesthood: A Living Sacrifice to God," the study addresses the partnership of pastors and priests with these observations: "The Lord has much to say in His Word about the responsibilities of the priests of God toward their pastors.... Let's explore together ways in

112

which the work of the Holy Ministry in your congregation and locale may be enhanced and be a joy—rather than a tedium—for your pastor." Of the seven listed passages, three feature admonitions to pay, two to respect, and two to pray for those who preach and teach.

Bottom-up Organizing

The opposite starting point is ably presented by Oscar Feucht, who for many years was secretary for adult education in the Lutheran Church—Missouri Synod. But first hear him describe what is wrong with undervaluing lay leaders.

> The average church member goes to church in the mood of a spectator instead of a participant. Yet Christians are part of God's orchestra! They are not called merely to give financial support to the orchestra but to play an instrument! A bishop in Manchester, England, put it tersely: "There has been in the past the impression that laymen exist 'to believe, to pray, to obey, and to pay.' " An American churchman has said: "The church faces ecclesiastical suicide unless it makes some radical changes in its traditional attitude toward laymen."[1]

Feucht's starting point is clear. The title of his CPH-published book is *Everyone a Minister.* The foundation is the priesthood of all believers. But that foundation can easily be obscured in church life. He says, "The priesthood of all Christians rests on a solid Biblical base, both in the New Testament and in the Old Testament. But this basic doctrine must be rediscovered by every new generation of Christians. Negatively stated, it can be lost in a single generation."[2]

Feucht approves this observation by William Dallmann:

> From justification by faith, it is an easy step to the universal priesthood of believers. The Old Testament distinction between priest and people, clergymen and laymen is at an end. Christ, our high priest, has made all Christians priests unto God. All Christians are God's clergy and so there is no special clerical order in the church. The ministry is an office, not an order, much less a threefold order of bishops, priests, deacons... The church is a government of the people, by the people, and for the people, and all Christians are the people.[3]

Another quote is from Elton Trueblood: "If we should take religion seriously as was done in the early Christian church, the dull picture presented by so many contemporary churches would be radically altered... pastors would not be performing while others watch, but helping to stir up the ministry of the ordinary members."[4]

Feucht highlights some half-truths often found in Lutheran tradition that work against a ministry of the laity. He asserts we will not build an active laity:

> if confirmation is a finishing school;
> if education is for children only;
> if mere church attendance is all that is required;
> if the impression is left that we have our faith "only to die by";
> if missions are for missionaries;
> if religion is something we delegate to our minister.[5]

Top-down Organizing

The top-down approach was evident in Christian churches already in the second century.[6] It is epitomized in the Roman Catholic Church today. The authority for churchly acts was given to the Apostle Peter and was passed on over the centuries through bishops to the individual priests properly ordained.

The issue is very much alive today in Lutheran circles, as the Evangelical Lutheran Church in America works to implement fellowship with the Episcopalian Church, the American version of the Church of England. Anglicans perpetuated apostolic succession after the official break with the Catholic Church of Rome.

Obviously many Lutherans find attractive the possibility of standing in the line of succession to that churchly authority passed from Christ to Peter and then down over the centuries through bishops. Symbolically this would certainly be a boost to morale and self image at a time when wide-spread discouragement is reported among pastors across all denominations.

But functionally the advantages are hard to identify, and dangers seem clear. The greatest concern should be unhealthy perpetuation of the two-caste thinking that divides clergy from laity. This is simply the wrong direction for the challenges facing Protestants at this time.

LUTHERAN PERSPECTIVES

The most thorough discussion of Lutheran approaches to ministry through the centuries from the Reformation to today's church bodies in America is offered by James Pragman in his CPH-published *Traditions of Ministry*.

He distinguishes between a narrow view of ministry and a broad view. Through the centuries the narrow view has been dominant. Seventeenth-century dogmatician Johann Gerhard presents it with the definition of the ministry of the church as "a sacred and public office, divinely instituted and committed to certain men through a legitimate calling" that gives them special power to teach the Word of God, to administer the sacraments, and to preserve discipline in the church.[7] The implication is that anyone else involved in ministry does so by delegation from the person ordained to this specially instituted office.

The broad view goes back to Luther himself as he dealt with the confusion that emerged as the Reformation extended to church life as well as to doctrine. If authority to preach the Gospel and administer the sacraments no longer flows from the pope, where does it come from? His answer was that all Christians are priests before God, and this priesthood of believers gathered as a congregation is the source of authority for the preaching of the Gospel and the administration of the sacraments in their midst. Luther taught that the office of preaching is the highest office in the church and by right it belongs to all believers. All ministries of the church belong to all Christians because they are each individually priests before God.[8]

Yet not all priests/ministers can do all the ministries at the same time. So the shared authority of the congregation is transferred to specific individuals to carry on in their name. They in effect delegate their power to one of them to function on their behalf. This congregational polity became basic to many Lutheran congregations and synods that had to begin on their own in America. Especially because of the moral and financial failure of their first self-styled bishop leader, the Lutherans who became the Missouri Synod insisted that church authority begin and remain in the individual congregations, rather than in the synod or convention that they freely choose to associate with.

This location of the source of authority in the congregation inevitably leads to uncertainty in its relationships to the synod and to the ordained pastor, both of which have authority of their own. The relationship of congregations to synod is undergoing major testing and reexamination at this time in the Missouri Synod. Reasons why congregations will exercise more autonomy and individuality were presented in the previous chapter. Greater diversity in worship, ministries, and church order is a fact of church life today, just as it is in most other institutions that are adjusting to constituents who expect their individual needs and preferences to be met.

The relationship between the authority of the congregation and that of the pastor is also under renewed discussion in the Missouri Synod, as it is in the Evangelical Lutheran Church in America. The relationship is certainly wrong when congregations treat their pastors as hired hands and also wrong when pastors treat their congregations as fiefdoms. The calling to spiritual leadership of a congregation is a special God-given responsibility that needs to be respected as something greater than the responsibility of all the other priests/ministers. With that special responsibility goes special authority in spiritual matters. But that authority cannot deprive the others of their own calling to minister.

The heritage of ethnic Lutheran churches from German and Scandinavian cultures includes unusually extensive authority for the village pastor. Those nineteenth-century cultures expressed top-down, paternalistic authoritarianism to a degree hard for modern Americans to imagine. The church was part of the state, and the pastor was a state-paid official who commanded considerable respect and obedience. "Spiritual authority" was extended into village life far more than would be tolerated today.

Nineteenth-century Lutheran pastors in America could be and were a different kind of church leader than pastors can be today. They typically served in a well defined, cohesive, foreign-language-speaking ethnic community of members who, by heritage, accepted and expected the pastor to tell them what they could and could not do. Their culture led them be passively obedient in their church life. "Der Herr Pastor" is the phrase frequently used to describe that style. That phrase usually reflects a negative to be overcome as Lutherans moved out of their ethnicity into mainstream American church life.

The priesthood of all believers was a valuable theological doctrine that helped congregations and church bodies in the new country to identify and establish their authority. But the implications of this doctrine were poorly realized in an inherited culture where ministry was what only "the minister" did.

Yet in God's providence the special heritage of the Lutheran Church—Missouri Synod is a congregational polity based on the priesthood of all believers. Social changes have brought the need for greater insistence on its implications. The theology is in place. Everybody is a minister. Churches that believe this behave differently. Congregations that get everyone into ministry are going to fulfill their mission better in today's culture.

Certainly pastors in such congregations have a distinctive, God-affirmed role that gives them special status deserving special respect. "Preacher" describes that status very well. Leave "minister" for all the other priests who have ministry to do.

APOSTOLIC ORGANIZING OF MINISTRY

The Apostle Paul based his organizing of ministry on two principles that were poorly understood in the centuries of Lutheran tradition. One is that every member of the fellowship is gifted by the Holy Spirit to contribute something special to the common good of the congregation. The other is that a basic task of the lead minister is to be a builder who equips the others to build up the fellowship that is their basic identity as a local congregation. Putting both principles to work can bring renewed life and energy to congregations that take them seriously.

Organizing Around Spiritual Giftedness

1 Corinthians 12 is Paul's clearest statement of the first principle. He starts: I want you to know the truth about gifts from the Holy Spirit. He explains: There are different kinds of spiritual gifts, different ways of serving, and different abilities to perform service; but the same Spirit, Lord, and God gives them all. The apostle presents a pivotal understanding for church leadership: The Spirit's presence is shown in some way in each person for the good of all. Paul, the foremost practitioner of apostolic style, underscores diversity: As the one Spirit wishes, he gives a different gift to each person.

In Romans 12 and Ephesians 4 the Apostle Paul presents more of his God-inspired teaching on spiritual gifts and their implications for church leadership.

If a church really believes that the Spirit motivates each member to contribute something special to the life of the congregation, then the organizing task revolves around identifying those contributions and helping members put them into service. These can range all the way from helping with simple tasks, to encouraging others, to healing, to giving funds in extra measure, to leadership and administration, to teaching, to proclaiming God's word. Paul also saw miraculous expressions of the Spirit among members. His message was simple: Whatever God has gifted you to do, do it.

117

The Apostle Peter worked with the same principle. He told the churches he led to manage those gifts well: "Each one, as a good manager of God's different gifts, must use for the good of others the special gift he has received from God" (1 Peter 4:10).

Clearly this is bottom-up organizing. Everyone has some service to contribute to the ministries of the congregation. The leadership task is to identify the giftedness of the members at hand and to get these various contributions employed so they can benefit all.

Recent generations of Lutherans in America have been accustomed to a different approach. This style relies on a carefully formulated set of constitutional by-laws to describe the ministries they want to provide. Usually a committee annually sets to work recruiting members for all the various positions their organizational plan calls for. In effect, people are fitted into pre-defined boxes for what their ministry is supposed to be. Sometimes there is a good match. Too often committees organized this way barely function for lack of interest among their members, and little gets done.

The principle of putting to work individual spiritual giftedness organizes in the opposite direction. Instead of fitting individuals into pre-determined boxes, organizational tasks are fitted to individuals. The result is that they contribute what they like to do and feel confident doing. Such interest and ability are basic evidence of spiritual giftedness. Instead of finding people to do jobs, the emphasis in this approach shifts to finding enough tasks to keep willing workers in ministry. The resulting structure is much messier than what can be logically described in by-laws. But the amount of ministry being done is usually higher.

Organizing around spiritual giftedness is the first apostolic principle. In application, real life in church organizations will be somewhere in-between starting with the tasks or starting with the workers. The second apostolic principle helps to bring focus and clarity to the resulting ambiguous and often-changing church structure.

Organizing To Build Up The Fellowship

A congregation is a structure of relationships between members. The Apostle Paul was very clear about what this structure should become and what the key leadership role should be. He liked to use the analogy of a physical building emerging under the leadership of a master builder.

"Like an expert builder, I laid a foundation and someone else is building on it," he says in 1 Corinthians 3:10. By trade he was a builder who made tents. As a carpenter, Jesus Christ was a builder, too. In congregational life

Paul saw himself building up a structure of tight-knit relationships between members sharing their life in Christ with each other. He saw himself building fellowship among God's people.

This builder analogy was by far his most-used description for his leadership role; it appears as verb or noun 32 times. The key word *oikodomeo* was commonly used at his time both in its literal sense of building a physical house and its figurative sense of building up a household of people who live in the building. That figurative sense of household can well be translated "fellowship" to describe the basic grouping of relationships in a local congregation. In the house churches of the New Testament the unit we call a congregation was really a household. Paul's work was all about building up fellowships, building up congregations.

To the Ephesians in the fourth chapter Paul made the clearest statement of his approach to organizing church life. God gave apostles, prophets, evangelists, pastors and teachers "to prepare God's people for works of service, so that the body of Christ may be built up" toward unity, maturity, and fullness of Christ. Certainly such leaders are to preach the Gospel and administer the Sacraments, which will always be fundamental to building up spiritual life. But there is much more to the task. They are to equip God's people for ministries that are to be shaped and guided toward building up the fellowship of a church. As Peter teaches, God's people "like living stones, are being built into a spiritual house to be a holy priesthood" (1 Peter 2:5).

There are many more practical and far-reaching implications for the apostolic principle of organizing ministry around the building up of living stones together into fellowship. They are discussed in my CPH-published book *New Designs for Church Leadership.*[9]

The main point here is what this emphasis on building means for the work and authority of the called and ordained pastors of a congregation. Theirs can be the role of the architect casting the vision and setting out the plan for the building of fellowship in that congregation.

In Lutheran tradition, pastors have functioned mostly as carpenters, or hands-on builders doing themselves such direct ministry tasks of presenting the Word, teaching, visiting the sick, encouraging those in need. When ministry is expanded to share those tasks with others, the pastor's special contribution becomes the higher-level leadership of a spiritual architect who preaches the framework for the spiritual life of a specific congregation, who teaches what that life can look like in practice, and who oversees the planning by which other member-builders can figure out how to contribute.

With everybody a minister, is much left for the pastor to do? In apostolic organizing there certainly is. Lively congregations need a vision of what they can become. Hearing the Gospel and receiving the sacraments are basic to how God generates the spiritual energy that makes a congregation come alive. The leader charged by God with guiding the spiritual life of the congregation is, in Paul's phrase, the logical master builder to discern and sketch out the vision for what that congregation's unique mixture of spiritual gifts, energy, and circumstances can become.

In apostolic style, every member is a builder, just like every member is a minister. To be the architect of this spiritual construction work is a unique privilege and responsibility.

ORGANIZING MORE
FLEXIBLE TRAINING FOR MINISTRY

If everyone in a congregation is a minister, then the church's responsibility to provide training for ministry expands considerably. It moves beyond traditional college and seminary training of full-time, called pastors and teachers. Many congregations with this bottom-up philosophy of ministry find themselves bringing specially gifted members on to part-time staff positions to train and lead volunteers in specialized ministries.

Common staff specialties are assimilation, evangelism, care giving, prayer, as well as more conventional children's ministry, youth leadership, and music. A congregation does not have to be very large to afford, say, a $5,000 director of assimilation who is enthused about this ministry for all the right reasons and who does not want to work full time. Going away for a year or two of college-level training is usually out of the question.

Such a person can become productive with on-the-job training. But in metropolitan areas churches can offer more thorough training by joining together in developing and offering appropriate course work locally, such as Bible, Lutheran doctrine, and practical ministry specialties. I am involved in developing such a program among LCMS churches in the Greater Cleveland area. This Ministry Specialist Training program is under the oversight of Concordia College in Ann Arbor, Michigan, which also sponsors the similar Parish Lay Specialist program of the Michigan District. The Northwest District, together with Concordia College in Portland, Oregon, is well along the way in offering training for lay ministers in remote parts of Alaska.

120

Another change in training perspective emerges with the realization that the work done by traditionally called pastors is largely a matter of spiritual giftedness. The Apostle Paul teaches this. Then perhaps some gifted church leaders with minimal course training might function as well and even better than many who have extensive graduate-level education. This observation suggests a model different from the accepted practice of first training prospective ministers in seminary and then having congregations engage them, often with disappointing results. A reasonable alternative is to have congregations first identify leaders of proven effectiveness in their midst and then bring to them formal course work that can strengthen their ministry while they continue doing it. This approach is closer to the apostolic style of raising up church leaders.

To consider non-traditional alternative paths to ministry does not deny the importance of conventional on-campus seminary programs. Such training will undoubtedly long remain the basic avenue into full-time, professional, ordained ministry as we know it. But the trend toward increasing diversity in how ministry is done by congregations calls into question how long seminaries can see themselves producing generalists for interchangeable parishes. The uniformity is especially apparent in preparation for leading worship. In 1998 Royal Redeemer, the congregation I serve, went through the synodical placement process of calling a seminary graduate who was expected to lead an established contemporary service. Informal inquiry discovered that only two of about 100 graduates had demonstrated such ability, and each was sought by at least four other congregations. Royal Redeemer had to turn elsewhere.

The direction it turned was toward bringing on staff full time a member of proven worship leadership skills, with the understanding he would gain ordination either through colloquy or through an innovative synod program called DELTO (Distance Education Leading to Ordination). This program has come under attack and has not initiated any training opportunities in the last two years. The future of this creative, far-sighted alternative avenue into ordained ministry is at present clouded.

The Missouri Synod was the fastest growing single grouping of Lutherans in America during the late 1800s and early 1900s. This outcome is usually credited to the ability of this association to provide more and better-trained ministers and teachers for the mushrooming number of congregations of immigrants sprouting up particularly in the mid-West. Such result in turn was attributable to investment especially between 1887 and 1906 in development of nine geographically spread *Gymnasia* (the

German version of high school and junior college) for the specialized purpose of preparing students for seminary.

The situation in the Missouri Synod today is almost the opposite. Many congregations are unable to find pastors prepared through traditional seminary training. One study shows that in the last ten years only half the number of ordained ministers who left the roster of active service have been replaced. With twice the number of congregations, the Evangelical Lutheran Church of America has four times the number of students enrolled in its seminaries. One estimate is that as many as 2,000 congregations of the Lutheran Church—Missouri Synod will be vacant by 2006.

Obviously something has to change if the Synod is to continue to meet the ministry needs of its congregations. Change is uncomfortable. But in the matter of training for ministry, changes in styles of organizing this necessary function are going to be unavoidable.

TOWARD BETTER ORGANIZING OF MINISTRY

The discussion of changing styles and unchanging Lutheran substance began ten years ago with the hope of understanding and promoting an infectious spirit of growth that has eluded most Lutheran congregations in recent decades. There is no one program or style that is going to pave the way. Christ's church remains a spiritual undertaking that human leaders try to guide and shape according to their understanding and circumstances. For faithful Lutherans this understanding needs to be based on God's word in Scripture. But Lutherans, like all Christians, bring to Scripture their own cultural assumptions and traditions about what a church should be and do.

Church culture, made up of those assumptions and traditions, can be a wonderful blessing. But it can also become a barrier to effective mission when the cultures of people they are trying to reach change and churches do not adapt.

When the line between necessary theological substance and changeable cultural expressions is unclear, purposeful change in styles can be very threatening. The intent in this book has been to narrow the most helpful cultural changes down to styles of communicating and styles of organizing.

Lutherans are used to looking to the written word of the apostles for necessary theological substance. The apostles' writings are also a good reference for ministry styles of communicating and organizing. Churches today that stay focused on the apostolic, New Testament church for substance and style will be most effective in negotiating transitions to new and changing cultures around them.

But ultimately human church leaders can deal with only part of the combination that keeps congregations healthy and energetic. It is the Holy Spirit who calls, gathers, enlightens and sanctifies the whole Christian church wherever it comes to expression. The Holy Spirit does not confine himself to just one church culture for all time. In times of social change, the path to faithfulness in ministry is to discern and follow the Spirit's lead toward changes in styles of communicating and organizing that offer promise for greater effectiveness in the unchanging mission of churches with Lutheran substance.

1 Oscar E. Feucht, *Everyone a Minister*, CPH 1974, p. 98

2 Feucht, p. 36.

3 Feucht, p. 34.

4 Feucht, p. 35.

5 Feucht, p. 98.

6 Greg Ogden, *The New Reformation: Returning the Ministry to the People of God*, Zondervan, 1990.

7 James H. Pragman, *Traditions of Ministry*, Concordia Publishing House, 1983, p. 62.

8 Pragman, p. 15.

9 David S. Luecke, *New Designs for Church Leadership*, Concordia Publishing House, 1990.